THAN

MW00426279

Special "thanks!" to the many people from these wonderful organizations who provided feedback and encouragement on this project:

Alliance Defending Freedom • ADF Foundation • American Bible Society • ABWE Foundation • Arctic Barnabas Ministries • African Enterprise • Azusa Pacific University • Baker Publishing Group • Barnabas Foundation • Best Christian Workplaces Institute • Bethany Christian Services • Billy Graham Evangelistic Association • Brewer Direct • Bridgeport Rescue Mission • Calvin College • Calvin Theological Seminary • CapinCrouse • Capital City Rescue Mission • Capital for Compassion • Catholic Health Services • Central Union Mission (Mission DC) • Chapel Point Church • Children at Heart Ministry • Christian Leadership Alliance • Christian Schools International • Christian Reformed Church in North America • City Gospel Mission (OH) • City Rescue Mission (FL) • City Rescue Mission (PA) • City Rescue Mission (OK) • City Union Mission • Cornerstone University • Covenant College • CRISTA Ministries • Dakota Boys and Girls Ranch • Daystar Television • Denver Rescue Mission • Design Group International • Dickerson Bakker & Associates • Douglas Shaw & Associates • Dutton Christian School • Evangelical Council for Financial Accountability • Evergreen Commons • Faith Comes By Hearing • 5by5 • Focus on the Family • Fresno Rescue Mission • Frey Resource Group • Frontier Camp • Galvin and Associates • The Gideons International • Global Bible Initiative • Grace Adventures • Grace Christian University • Grandville Calvin Christian Schools • Guiding Light Mission • Gull Lake Ministries • Halo Ministry • Haven of Rest Ministries (OH) • Haven of Rest Ministries (SC) • Helping Up Mission • Holland Christian Schools • Holland Home Foundation • Holland Rescue Mission • John 3:16 Mission • Judson University • Kalamazoo Gospel Mission • Kent Communications, Inc. •

Keys for Kids Ministries • Kuyper College • Landmark Christian School • Los Angeles Mission • Las Vegas Rescue Mission • Leadership Ministries Worldwide • Lexington Rescue Mission • Life 102.5/Faith 1190 (WI) • Life Action Ministries • Life on the Edge • Ligonier Ministries • Living Water International • Love INC (MO) • Masterworks • MB Foundation • Mel Trotter Ministries • Memphis Union Mission • Mercy Ships • Meyer Partners, LLC • Miami Rescue Mission • Milwaukee Direct Marketing • Miracle Hill Ministries • Mission Aviation Fellowship • Mission India • Mission Resource Alliance • Mission To Children • Moja Marketplace • Moline Christian School • Muncie Mission Ministries • Muskegon Rescue Mission • The Navigators • Navigator Church Ministries • National Christian Foundation • New Life Academy • New York City Rescue Mission • Nimble Connect • Northern Michigan Christian Schools • One & All • The Orchard Foundation • The Other Way Ministries • Open Door Mission • Our Daily Bread Ministries • Overseas Council • Pacific Garden Mission • Partners Worldwide • Phoenix Christian Preparatory School • Phoenix Rescue Mission • The Potter's House Christian School • Precept Ministries International • Pregnancy Resource Center of Grand Rapids • Ratio Christi • Release Ministries • Rescue Mission Alliance • Rockford Rescue Mission • Saint Mary's University in Minnesota • Saint Matthews House • Salina Rescue Mission • Samaritan's Purse • The Salvation Army • San Diego Rescue Mission • The Seed Company • The Sending Project • 98.5 KTIS (MN) • Senior Neighbors, Inc. • South Christian High School • Southern New Hampshire Rescue Mission • Springfield Rescue Mission • Springs Rescue Mission • Star of Hope Mission • Streams of Hope • Sunday Breakfast Mission • The Timothy Group • Trinity Christian College • Union Gospel Mission (TX) • Union Gospel Mission (OR) • The Union Mission Ministries • Unlimited Grace Media • Visalia Rescue Mission • Water Street Mission • Wedgwood Christian Services • White's Residential and Family Services • Winston-Salem Rescue Mission • World Impact • World Renew • World Vision International • Wycliffe Bible Translators

RIDE
THE
WAVE

EXPERIENCE HISTORY'S BIGGEST FLOW OF
WEALTH AND WORSHIP WITH ESTATE GIFTS

MIKE BUWALDA
FOUNDER OF MONEY FOR MINISTRY

Ride the Wave
Copyright © 2018 by Money for Ministry LLC

All right reserved.

Published in the United States by Money for Ministry LLC,
Grand Rapids, Michigan

For more information, please visit *moneyforministry.com*

ISBN: 978-1-5323-7084-7

Special Thanks to:
Cover and Interior Design: Frank Gutbrod
Editing Team: Amber Brandt, Keith Meyering, Mark Tremaine,
Cindy Hendricks, Doug Bouws, Dan Hubka, and Judy Flier
Author Advisors: Ron Haas, Clare DeGraaf, Curt Harding,
Andrew Olsen, and Ted Boers
Cartoons: Nate Buwalda
Book Finances: Joanie Comeaux
Promotion: Dan Hubka and Lisa Fulton
Printing and Fulfillment: Our Daily Bread Ministries

Printed in the United States of America
First edition

TABLE OF CONTENTS

139 CLOSING THOUGHTS
WAVES OF JOY
5 Keys to Ride the Wave Now

INTRODUCTION

WAVES OF LIME GREEN SHERBET

How my eyes were opened to history's biggest flow of wealth and worship

feel like the *least* qualified person on the planet to talk to you about estate gifts.

I'm not an attorney, an accountant, or a financial advisor.

But I am a *messenger* whose eyes were opened by God years ago to a stunning reality: ministry organizations worldwide were leaving millions and even billions of estate gift dollars on the table during the largest generational wealth transfer in history. And I was just foolish and naïve enough to believe God could use me to do something about it.

And God has certainly come through over the years, stirring within me a passion and confidence in the powerful and peace-producing truth found in 1 Corinthians 3 — that if we are faithful in planting seeds, and watering them, then we can trust God for the growth.

We can trust God to make waves.
We can trust God for more estate gifts.
We can trust God to work in the hearts of our donors.
Can I get an Amen?

Since that revelation, the Lord has worked through me and our amazing team of called and committed fellow travelers at Money for Ministry to help surface over $600 million in estate gifts as of this writing for the cause of Christ.

We work in partnership with many Christian nonprofits like yours, and have witnessed thousands upon thousands of ministry-minded donor prospects expressing interest in "leaving a legacy" and considering their largest gift ever — a charitable gift in their Will.

MINISTRY ORGANIZATIONS ARE LEAVING MILLIONS OF ESTATE GIFT DOLLARS ON THE TABLE DURING THE LARGEST GENERATIONAL WEALTH TRANSFER IN HISTORY.

This tidal wave of activity we're witnessing has opened many exciting doors for kingdom impact, including two nationally recognized ministries that have each asked our team to help them reach $1 billion estate gift goals. And here we are today, like Abraham, obeying and walking by faith, as we dream and pray about the possibility of how God could use us to join hands with our growing list of ministry friends and surface $5 billion of estate gifts for kingdom impact over the next 10 years.

Believe it or not, this incredible and unlikely journey all began with lime green sherbet.

My first job out of college was serving as a development director for a Christian school in Northern Michigan. I honestly didn't even know what a development director was when I applied for the position, but quickly fell in love with how the role combined two passions God had been stirring in me throughout my college years: ministry and marketing.

BELIEVE IT OR NOT THIS INCREDIBLE AND UNLIKELY JOURNEY ALL BEGAN WITH LIME GREEN SHERBET.

My first task on the job was to create a large-scale auction event. Our leadership had a conversation with a Catholic school in a larger city nearby to discover what had made their auction such a massive success. The Catholic school was very gracious, and shared their secret: a wet bar and a raffle. While we appreciated their candor, we just weren't sure how to apply this advice at our conservative, rural school.

I'm happy to say that even without employing the other school's formula for success, our inaugural auction was a big hit. When the dust settled, we had actually exceeded our fundraising goal.

Soon after, the superintendent gave me a report that listed a handful of estate gifts the school had received in recent years. We immediately noticed that a single estate gift almost always produced more revenue than our labor-intensive auction did. That really got my attention!

> ESTATE GIFTS WERE GIVING US OUR BEST RETURN ON TIME AND MONEY.

The auction took months of coordination, meetings and countless volunteer hours to pull off. The estate gift, on the other hand, required little or even no effort on our part. Now, I'm no math expert, but it seemed like the estate gifts were giving us our best return on time and money.

So the obvious question became: how do we get *more* of these mysterious estate gifts?

I set out to find the answer. My first call was to our good friends and gift planning experts at Barnabas Foundation. Our school was a member of Barnabas Foundation, so they offered to send one of their expert gift planners to share about stewardship and legacy giving with our community of supporters if I would organize an event.

It was summertime, and I began to feel anxious as I wondered what would inspire people to sacrifice a beautiful summer evening with their families to come hear an attorney talk about estate gifts — in a school cafeteria with no windows, no air conditioning and uncomfortable bench seating.

My "genius" solution? Let's entice them with lime green sherbet in little Styrofoam cups!

Now, be honest. Can you imagine a more powerful or compelling marketing strategy than that? Me either. So I typed up invitation letters on the school's letterhead and mailed them to several of our longtime faithful donors, figuring they'd be the people most likely to come.

> WHAT WOULD INSPIRE PEOPLE TO SACRIFICE A BEAUTIFUL SUMMER EVENING TO HEAR AN ATTORNEY TALK ABOUT ESTATE GIFTS?

The evening came and I was pleasantly surprised to see so many people show up ... And they were *smiling,* despite the humidity! So with little beads of sweat on their foreheads, they enjoyed a complimentary cup of lime green sherbet and learned how to create or update their Wills, and (hopefully) include our school in their estate planning.

Over the next few years, I began to pay more attention to these families who had come to learn about estate gifts. I followed up with some of them, and if they were interested, arranged for them to meet with a Barnabas Foundation gift planner.

I kept my thumb on the pulse of what was happening and the kind of results we were getting. I was amazed to learn that these faithful "under the radar" givers, many of whom were giving less than $500 a year to the school, were committing *100 times that much* (ex. $50,000) to the school in their estate plans.

THIS IS ABOUT SO MUCH MORE THAN WEALTH. IT'S ABOUT A SPECIAL ACT OF WORSHIP CALLED ESTATE GIFTS THAT GOD IS USING TO SHARE HIS LOVE WITH THE WORLD.

What was going on?

I wasn't exactly sure. But the obvious next step for me was to start buying more cups of sherbet.

Since that very humble beginning, the Lord has taken me and our Money for Ministry team on an incredible adventure to discover how Christ-centered nonprofits can maximize the number of estate gifts they receive during this historical generational transfer of wealth. And in the process, we've learned it's about so much more than wealth. It's about a special act of worship called estate gifts that God is using to fuel our common desire to share His love with the world.

After my time working for that Christian school, I went on to serve for several years at an international relief and development ministry, before launching Money for Ministry. Over the past 15 years since, the Lord has opened many doors for my team and I to serve a wide range of ministry organizations.

We've been honored to partner with overseas missions, K-12 schools, colleges and universities, seminaries, rescue missions that serve homeless individuals, Bible study and distribution organizations, Catholic charities, youth ministries, religious freedom, senior care, evangelism and discipleship, and more. And we've had the privilege of working in partnership with some of the most respected ministry associations, gift planners, agencies, and consulting companies in our field.

Through these experiences, I've sensed God leading me to share what we've been learning along the way on this kingdom-impacting journey — the "best of the best" approaches we see the Lord blessing over and over again.

> THIS BOOK IS A COLLECTION OF THE "BEST OF THE BEST" APPROACHES WE SEE THE LORD BLESSING.

Within these pages, you'll find proven growth tips, mistakes to avoid, frequently asked questions, ingredients for a successful game plan, insights from your peers on the front lines of ministry, and much more. We pray the information you're about to read will help you make the most of this historical moment, and serve the hearts of your donors well, and see more estate gifts than ever before.

So buckle up — this is going to be fun!

WHAT'S WORKING
A WORSHIP MINDSET

"At its core, giving that supports Kingdom work is a reverent act of loving worship. This truth holds true for near-term outright giving, and for planned legacy bequest giving. Bearing powerful witness to this are the many, many faithful examples we see of legacy gifts entrusted to support Missions for generations to come."

Lee Manis
American Bible Society

Donor Dan regretted his request for more information on creative planned giving options.

1

THE WAVE OF INSPIRATION OVER INFORMATION

Speak to their hearts before you speak to their heads

ave you ever been with an older family member who starts sharing all of the gory details of their recent medical procedure? Without fail, everyone breathes a sigh of relief when someone finally holds up their hand and says with a smile, "Stop! T.M.I — too much information!"

Like our older relatives, ministry leaders often do the same thing, sharing *way* too much information about planned giving. And I get it.

The companies that sell planned gift marketing websites, for example, need to justify the cost of their comprehensive content. So they load up the sites with countless pages and links, hoping the average development director or ministry board will glance over it and conclude it must be a smart investment.

But now think about this from the perspective of your donors. Or better yet, let's make it really personal and imagine one of your older relatives relaxing at home in the evening, deciding how to spend their free time. Do you have someone in mind?

Now ask yourself: would that relative of mine ever in a million years say, "You know, that ministry I support has an incredible planned giving website with over 100 pages of articles and tools. Come to think of it, I've been meaning to read through all that content so I can become an expert on all of the options available to me. I'm going to grab my favorite drink and wade through that website tonight!"

> MINISTRIES SPEND THOUSANDS OF DOLLARS ON THE FALSE PREMISE THAT WHAT DONORS REALLY WANT IS MORE PLANNED GIVING INFORMATION.

Ridiculous, right? But that's the crazy bet countless ministries have unknowingly made. Or maybe a planned giving website is all they know to do, so they end up spending thousands of dollars on the false premise that what their donors really want and need is more planned giving information. "We need to educate our donors," they say with great conviction.

They have good intentions, but they end up with pages and pages of mind-numbing content like the example below (and by the way, I'm not making this up, this is real verbiage from an actual ministry's planned gift marketing materials):

A unitrust differs from an annuity trust in that distributions are based on a fixed percentage of the net fair market value of the trust assets, as determined on a specified day of each year of the unitrust. While the percentage is fixed (again, it cannot be less than 5%), the value of the unitrust assets fluctuates each year. As a result, unitrust payments increase as the value of the trust assets increase, and decrease as the value of the trust assets decrease. When you create the trust, you specify the percentage of the unitrust's net fair market value that is to be distributed each year.

Huh?! I almost fell asleep just *typing* that paragraph for you!

To make matters worse, nonprofits often don't stop after providing super boring definitions and details like this. They go a step further to provide their donors with "bonus" content such as sterile tax tips, practical living strategies for seniors, made-up generic donor stories, charts and graphs detailing how various planned gift instruments work, and much more — all written in confusing legal jargon no average person can understand.

All of this information does *nothing* for your estate gift growth, (but if you're having trouble sleeping at night and want to avoid expensive treatment plans for insomnia, it may be cheaper to just read through some planned gift marketing materials!)

GIVE YOUR DONORS SOME INSPIRATION FIRST, THEN FOLLOW WITH HOW-TO INFORMATION IF THEY'RE INTERESTED.

What donors really want and need first isn't information but *inspiration*. Making an estate gift is actually an emotional decision. For many, it is an expression of their love for the Lord and their families. It represents a lifetime of memories and feelings about their spouse, their kids, their grandkids, their church, their work, and more. It's fueled by joy and a desire to bless people beyond their lifetimes.

So please don't lead with *information* about gift planning techniques. Or tax tips, or tools and calculators, or a glossary of terms. Lead with *inspiration* that engages people's greatest aspirations and deepest passions. You'll quickly discover that for most people, their family and their faith will be the ultimate inspiration to consider taking action on an estate gift. Focus your message there.

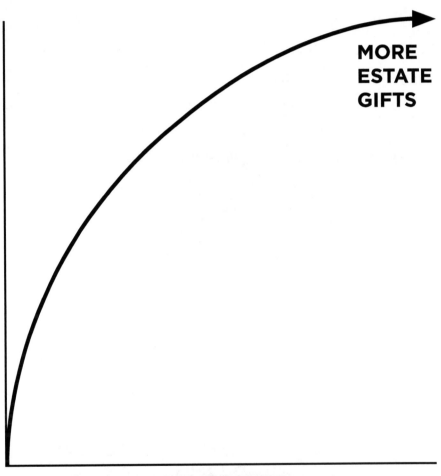

MORE
ESTATE
GIFTS

INSPIRATION

FREQUENTLY ASKED QUESTIONS

Q **What's the best way to explain to our donors how various planned gift instruments work?**

If you're asking questions like this, let me break it to you gently: you're probably on the wrong track, my friend!

Let me illustrate with an example.

A well-known national ministry recently lamented to me, "We think our planned gift stuff sounds like a lawyer and an accountant wrote them."

"What do you mean by that?" I prodded.

They went on to explain how important it is to them that all of their donor communications reflect the heart and soul of their ministry — changed lives in the name of Christ. They were so pleased to report that everything their development team had crafted in recent years met that standard, except for their planned giving materials. "It just doesn't sound like *us*," they observed.

For starters, we took a look at their website and quickly discovered that all of the content was built around the very common but ineffective "terminology and techniques" approach. We found carefully-crafted lists of various planned gift instruments, the advantages and tax implications of these instruments, and charts to show how these gift planning options work. If it had been a college research paper, the professor would have been very proud and given them an A.

But this was not an academic exercise to impress a professor. It was about a huge database of real donors who loved their ministry. And they discovered the hard way that these donors could actually care less about their expertise in the fine points of planned giving.

So our team recommended they build their approach around the two things we knew their donors cared most about:

THIS IS NOT AN ACADEMIC EXERCISE. THIS IS ABOUT REAL DONORS WHO LOVE YOUR MINISTRY.

their faith in Christ and their families (ex. spouse, kids, grandkids). We call this our "faith and family" approach. And we've found that donors love it, because we are speaking in easy-to-understand language that resonates with the deepest desires of their hearts.

I know this works because Money for Ministry has engaged thousands and thousands of ministry-minded donors on this topic. When we ask them about their motivation for giving and why they might even consider including a ministry in their Wills, it has almost nothing to do with tax savings or a desire for more information about smart gift planning strategies.

Instead, the motivation is a sense that they've been blessed by God over the years, and are therefore willing to return a portion of that blessing back to God as an offering of thanks.

In other words, for a majority of ministry-minded donors, an estate gift is an act of worship — not just a legal transaction or an efficient financial maneuver. Donors give from a deep conviction and an overflowing sense of gratitude that their lives and families are a gift from the hand of God. A gift in their Will then becomes a tangible way of saying "thank you!" to God for a lifetime of blessing. (Doesn't that just give you tingles up and down your spine?)

So then, if worship, gratitude, faith and family are the motivations that drive most charitable estate gifts, why do so many ministries lead with articles and brochures that emphasize the "terminology and techniques" of planned giving? It's not hard to find lifeless titles such as *Everything You've Always Wanted to Know about Charitable Remainder Trusts* or *The ABC's of Bequests, Wills, and Trusts*. But it doesn't have to be this way — there's no rule that says you have to be boring!

FOR A MAJORITY OF MINISTRY-MINDED DONORS, ESTATE GIFTS ARE AN ACT OF WORSHIP.

It probably doesn't come as a surprise that Money for Ministry recommends you flip the traditional approach around 180 degrees and lead instead with inspirational "faith and family" titles like *Becoming the Person God Made You to Be* or *How to Avoid a Family Landmine*. This approach connects with people on an emotional 'heart' level, and opens the door for you to introduce the estate gift topic in a reader-friendly way.

> FAITH AND FAMILY MESSAGING CONNECTS WITH MINISTRY-MINDED DONORS ON AN EMOTIONAL HEART LEVEL.

The aspirational "faith and family" mindset resonates with Christian nonprofit leaders because it taps into the reason they got into vocational ministry in the first place — a deep sense of calling from the Lord to serve the body of Christ and see it flourish.

The other reason they love the "faith and family" approach is more practical — it flat out gets such a better response than the traditional "terminology and techniques" approach. In fact, a well-respected ministry we work with decided to test this — without telling us! They offered the "terminology and techniques" content they'd been using with half their prospect pool.

Then they offered our recommended "faith and family" content to the other half of the pool. Can you guess what happened? The requests for "faith and family" content were *10 times greater* than their conventional "terminology and techniques" materials! We've worked with this ministry for several years, and the response to planned gift materials that "sound like us" remains strong year after year.

We have a *really* cool planned giving website. We're all set now, right?

If your only goal is to "check a box" and tell your boss you've got the planned giving bases covered, then yes, an information-heavy website may be all you need. But be aware that if you're relying on your website to be the heart of your planned gift marketing strategy, you'll experience three (totally correctable) limitations:

1. Planned Giving Websites Usually Emphasize *Content* over *Conversions*. The number one limitation of cool planned giving websites is that they focus on *content* rather than *conversions*. A content focus means you may have over 100 impressive-looking pages about how a charitable lead trust works, or a detailed analysis of how an IRA rollover gift would play out in different tax brackets, or even practical living advice for seniors about how to save money in retirement.

But at the end of the day, how many people are actually "converting" online and including your ministry in their Wills?

Whenever we ask how many people are converting online, the answer from most ministries is either "we don't know" or "very few." In fact, one large national ministry we've worked with went 10 years before they noticed that their very cool content-rich website was barely getting *any* clicks, let alone any real conversion results.

Turns out someone had sold them on the idea that a "robust" planned giving website was the way to go. And so they dutifully built it, hoping donors would come. When I asked for a report of how many donors had actually did come to their site, the soothing sound of crickets filled the room.

CREATE CONTENT THAT INSPIRES RESPONDERS RATHER THAN INFORMS READERS.

You can avoid this very common mistake by creating content that *inspires responders* rather than *informs readers*. One of the best ways to accomplish this is to speak to the "faith and family" needs and desires of your audience, then simply ask for a response such as "Would you ever consider including us in your Will?"

2. Planned Giving Websites Ignore the "Senior Suspicion" Factor. The average age of a ministry marketing staff member is 35. The average age of a donor who passes away and leaves an estate gift is 85. A 50-year difference! That means there are at least two generations between the people *leading* and those *reading* your planned gift messaging. Do you see a potential problem here?

We see this all the time in numerous ministry organizations: talented, tech savvy marketing people making planned gift marketing decisions that resonate with their own personal online experiences and preferences, but are often unintentionally disconnected from the reality of how older seniors engage (or don't engage) online.

For example, if a marketing director likes Facebook or Instagram, they may enjoy scrolling through their smartphone throughout the day for updates, and maybe even assume that most of their donors are doing the same. And for a growing segment of their donor base, this may be true.

But, for estate gift donors (you know, the ones who will be responsible for the largest wealth transfer in history!), the reality is they actually have a 70 percent preference for correspondence through the *mail.* I know, that seems almost impossible to believe!

But we know this to be true from studying tons of internal data, which is based on our first-hand experience engaging thousands

> THERE ARE OFTEN TWO GENERATIONS BETWEEN THE PEOPLE LEADING AND READING PLANNED GIFT MESSAGING.

and thousands of older ministry donors about estate gifts. They want to hold a piece of paper in their hands. They like to respond through the mail. And their perception of materials that come through the mail is that they are more credible and more important than digital communications.

This reality often makes marketing people in their 30s and 40s scratch their heads in amazement, because a preference for physical mail over digital communication sounds so old-school and out of date. And it just doesn't compute in the world they live in, where everyone is up to

MOST ESTATE GIFT DONORS PREFER CORRESPONDENCE THROUGH THE MAIL.

speed with the newest smart phones, the latest apps, and the most cutting edge online productivity tools.

But now take just a minute and try to see this from the point of view of your older donors.

The reason many of these faithful friends have ventured into the scary world of the Internet in the first place was because their adult children wanted to communicate with them by email, and their grandkids were all on social media. So they reluctantly joined their families online, and soon discovered the joys of surfing the web for themselves — news sites, YouTube videos, online games, and more.

But your older donors remain somewhat suspicious of the Internet — especially when it comes to discussing sensitive, personal financial planning topics. And can you blame them? We've all seen the headlines where a major credit reporting agency experiences a massive data breach exposing the personal information of millions of Americans.

Your older donors are most certainly taking note of stories like this that confirm their suspicions about the Internet, causing them to become even more cautious about engaging with anyone online concerning financial planning topics.

> MANY OLDER DONORS ARE TAKING NOTE OF NEWS STORIES THAT CONFIRM THEIR SUSPICIONS ABOUT THE INTERNET.

So what are ministries doing? Unfortunately, many fail to recognize the trends we've been discussing and continue down the path that is most familiar and exciting to them — placing even *more* of their planned gift marketing emphasis online. For example, we've come across a fairly popular online planned gift marketing tool offering to help donors plan their legacy.

Sounds great until you start clicking through and realize seniors are being asked to enter their personal contact information — and even their social security number! I will say, it's a nice-looking tool, and I can see why marketing and fundraising teams would like it, but can you begin to see why this kind of approach is so out of touch with the people you most need to reach?

3. Planned Giving Websites can bog you down in reams of time-wasting meaningless data. Left-handed male university students in Honduras who drink Coke products are spending an average of 9 minutes each on your Planned Giving Tools page, and 2 percent of them clicked on your "Contact Us" link!

Very interesting, right? But how would you ever *use* this information to help your ministry grow?

It amazes me how often ministry leaders ask about planned giving website analytics, especially since this is not where the vast majority of actual estate gift growth is taking place. Sure, web analytic data is exciting and of interest to development teams, but it's not where most of your estate gift donors live.

What you ultimately want are more legacy givers and qualified, interested prospects, right? So then, where *do* they come from?

> MANY MINISTRY LEADERS ARE FASCINATED BY WEB SIGHT ANALYTICS-EVEN THOUGH THAT'S NOT WHERE MOST ESTATE GIFT GROWTH IS HAPPENING.

Here you go: as we mentioned above, the hands-down, first-place winner is *mail-back correspondence* (with personal contacts and online marketing coming in a distant second and third place, respectively). We have seen this reality play out over and over again as we've tested and observed a wide range of multi-channel approaches with ministries.

In fact, a research paper from a planned gift marketing company that specializes in online services confirmed the same thing: as much as we all love digital marketing and hope it will someday be the lead horse in this race, direct response in the physical mail is still the engine driving much of the actual estate gift results. From everything we're seeing, we expect this trend to continue for another 5-10 years.

> **DIRECT RESPONSE PHYSICAL MAIL IS STILL THE ENGINE DRIVING MUCH OF ACTUAL ESTATE GIFT RESULTS.**

Another reason I'm amazed by the fascination with planned giving website analytics is that many of the ministries who ask about them don't yet even have a good system for tracking or analyzing their existing ministry website traffic. And yet when it comes to planned giving, they expect detailed reporting to prove that it's "working."

Unfortunately, most planned giving website vendors know this — and are happy to supply their clients with lots of beautiful but meaningless detailed statistics. For example, a ministry leader recently sent me pages of data they had collected over several years tracking their website traffic.

I was impressed with the amount of granular detail this respected national vendor supplied to its nonprofit clients. But what impressed me more, was that nothing of any consequence was actually happening online. To quote Shakespeare, it was a lot of "sound and fury, signifying nothing."

So what's the solution? If your ministry is putting all (or most) of its planned giving hopes in a cool website, what can you do to position yourself to ride the wave and see more estate gifts than ever before? Our team at Money for Ministry recommends two proven approaches:

Focus on two measurements. The best way to avoid the temptation of getting sidetracked with relatively meaningless website data is to focus your planned gift marketing analysis on two measurements: new legacy givers and newly interested prospects.

If you want to improve how you track interest online, we recommend you begin your analysis with whatever tool your ministry already uses to evaluate your overall web traffic (ex. Google Analytics). Once that is in place, there are several ministry-tested ways you can proactively generate interest and leads.

You can post a feature article on your home page for maximum visibility that links to some "faith and family" content. Or add a checkbox for an inspirational brochure on your donation page.

> FOCUS ON TWO
> MEASUREMENTS:
> NEW LEGACY
> GIVERS
> AND NEWLY
> INTERESTED
> PROSPECTS.

And if you want to track individual donors who are expressing interest online, we recommend you use an email marketing program (ex. Mailchimp, AWeber or Constant Contact). This allows you to not only deliver your best "faith and family" content directly to donors, but also provides a report of who is clicking on that content.

See your website as part of a larger whole. We recommend you see your website as a *part* (not the whole) of an overall game plan. We love creating and updating content for planned giving websites. We love helping ministries explore creative and proven ways to drive more traffic to their sites.

But we also want you to realize up front that this is not where you're going to get the biggest bang for your buck. To maximize your God-given estate gift potential, you'll want to use your website as a supporting rather than primary part of a proven 5-part game plan (more on how to do this in the last chapter):

1. **Goal to Keep You Going**
2. **Message for the Masses**
3. **Interaction with the Interested**
4. **Connection with the Committed**
5. **Traction with Your Team**

Q How come no one is responding to the planned giving checkboxes on our reply slips and receipts?

The short answer is they probably need to first be inspired, not informed.

The other day I asked a ministry what they were doing to promote planned giving. The development director said he was putting checkboxes on his receipts and reply slips that said "I have already included your ministry in my Will" and "I would like more information about planned giving."

I first congratulated him for being proactive and including those checkboxes, because many ministries and direct mail agencies wouldn't want to include *anything* about planned giving in their direct mail appeals or receipts (which usually include a request for the next gift).

The reason they typically stay away from this kind of smart, planned gift integration is because they fear it will have a negative effect on their current fundraising efforts. Experience, however, has proven that the opposite is actually true — planned gift ministry integration has a very positive impact on current and future fundraising (more on that in chapter 4).

If you're already convinced that integrating planned giving into your direct response mail appeals is a good idea, but you're struggling to improve your response rate, start by asking if there is any inspiration for your donors to respond to. Then look at how the information is presented.

To make this really practical, there are four things we recommend you consider when it comes to reply slips in mail appeals:

Approach. Instead of just *asking* your donors if they've included you in their Will, try *giving* them something of value to begin the conversation. When you begin by asking estate gift prospects if they are ready to take action on an estate gift, you are appealing to a very small percentage of your donor file.

> OFFER TO GIVE PEOPLE SOMETHING ON YOUR RESPONSE CARDS — NOT JUST ASK THEM FOR SOMETHING.

But if you offer them something they may find inspiring, helpful, or encouraging (ex. a piece entitled "How to Bless Your Family for Generations to Come"), you've appealed to a much wider audience, and gone about it the right way — offer *inspiration* which earns you the right to introduce the "leave a legacy" theme in the *information* you send them.

Wording. The other big mistake the Money for Ministry team sees is how the checkbox response offer is worded. For example, if it reads "I would like more information about planned giving," you've already missed the vast majority of your audience, as the research shows that nearly 70 percent of active donors don't recognize the phrase "planned giving."

Placement. More often than not, the planned gift checkbox is buried on the backside of the reply device or receipt letter in small print underneath the small-print credit card gift information. In other words, your donors certainly aren't feeling inspired and probably never even saw it!

Expectations. We love integrating planned gift response offers into the direct mail stream along with receipt letters. Our team recommends this all the time, collaborates with various direct response agencies on unique ways to integrate them, and loves to hear the stories of how donors are responding and ministries are tracking those responses.

But having said that, we caution ministries against having too high of expectations with this approach. Planned gift checkboxes in reply devices and receipts are what we call a "piggyback approach" which means they are not the focal point, but rather simply coming along for the ride.

We advise you to consider the check-box strategy as a nice addition to your overall marketing mix, but not the main driver of your responses and results. To put this in context, if your approach, placement and wording are good, you might expect to see one response for every 1,000 planned gift checkboxes in receipts and reply devices.

RECAP

HOW TO RIDE THE WAVE OF INSPIRATION OVER INFORMATION

Give your donors some inspiration first, then follow with how-to information if they're interested.

For a majority of ministry-minded donors, estate gifts are an act of worship.

Create content that inspires responders rather than informs readers.

Estate gift donors prefer correspondence through the mail.

Focus on two metrics: new legacy givers and newly interested prospects.

Use your website within the context of an overall 5-part game plan (see last chapter for more on this).

Offer to give people something on your response cards — not just ask them for something.

Replace jargon like "planned giving" or "bequest" with clear everyday words like "gift in my Will".

Put your planned gift checkboxes on the front side directly underneath the donation options.

Aim for one response per 1,000 checkboxes (assuming good approach, placement, and wording).

WHAT'S WORKING
FAITH AND FAMILY MESSAGING

" Faith and family messaging is what resonates with donors because it speaks steadfastly to their heart and soul. It's what's important to them. We've used this approach in our messaging, surveys, and multi-channel marketing strategy and it has produced phenomenal results — with response rates over 20 percent. Our Goodheart Legacy Society has grown by 56 percent, and our prospect pool is now more like a lake than a backyard kiddie pool!"

Alice Cavanaugh
Denver Rescue Mission

Fundraiser Frank enjoyed sharing his favorite
planned gift ideas and stories with Donor Diane.

2

THE WAVE OF DIALOGUE OVER MONOLOGUE

A conversation with friends beats advertising to strangers

ichael Phelps is the most successful and decorated Olympian of all time, earning a total of 28 medals. Much of his success has been attributed to his consistent and ambitious workout routine — swimming up to 50 miles per week. With four years between each Olympic Games, that adds up to about 10,000 miles of swimming practice to help him win the gold!

Now what do you suppose would have happened if Michael Phelps didn't have a workout routine? What if Michael had told his coach, "I'm only going to practice one day per year. Give me the best workouts and exercises you have, and I'll give you everything I've got for that one-day workout per year."

As talented as Michael is, you know his one-day-per-year workout idea wouldn't work. He probably wouldn't win any races, let alone his historic 28 medals.

It sounds crazy, but this is exactly how many Christian nonprofits approach their planned gift growth. They essentially give it their best shot once a year and say things like:

> *"Let's do a special planned gift mailing every year in June."*
> *"Let's include planned giving in our capital campaign."*
> *"Let's add a checkbox to all of our receipt inserts in*
> *December so people can tell us if we're in their Will."*

I call this the "one and done" *monologue* approach. It's fueled by very good intentions — and I do applaud these ministries for doing *something* instead of *nothing* with planned giving. But the "one and done" monologue approach doesn't work because it's totally out of sync with how people actually decide to make an estate gift.

Unlike everything else you do in fundraising where *you* control the timing (ex. direct mail and e-mail appeals, special events, major donor visits, etc.), estate gifts are almost always triggered by the timing of the *donor* — specifically, unpredictable life events. Such as:

- **Family changes** (ex. death, marriage, remarriage, divorce, kids, grandkids, etc.)
- **Health changes** (ex. hospitalization, surgery, cancer diagnosis, heart attack, etc.)
- **Finance changes** (ex. selling a home, selling the business, fixed income, moving to a senior care facility, etc.)

These unpredictable life events are often the moment where people stop and say "You know, I think *now* is the time for me to create or update my Will." So if your "one and done" monologue mailing comes in June, and your donor's unpredictable life event happens in November, you likely missed the opportunity.

Instead, we recommend you use the highly-effective approach of creating an ongoing *dialogue* with your donors about leaving a legacy and including your ministry in their Wills. Because estate gift prospects have such a strong preference for mail-back correspondence, this *dialogue* doesn't necessarily mean you'll even speak to the donor in person.

In fact, for the majority of new estate gift donors and interested prospects that our team helps ministries surface, the donors moved from awareness to interest to action through ongoing mail-back correspondence alone — without ever interacting with the development team in person!

Unlike major donors that are used to high touch personal treatment, many estate givers actually *prefer* holding a piece of paper in their hands and initiating their response by mail if they're interested. Your approach then should be a series of communications that inspire people, ask for a response, offer help, repeat. In short, treat your planned gift messaging like a warm, ongoing conversation with friends rather than a commercial you broadcast to faceless strangers once a year.

This ongoing warm "conversation" (mostly in the mail) is the key to your ministry surfacing more estate gifts than ever before. Money for Ministry has guided many ministries through this process. Many leaders like you told us they found it challenging to set this up and maintain it in-house, so we built an automated system to help ministries maximize their estate gift results with minimum staff time.

> TREAT YOUR PLANNED GIFT MESSAGING LIKE A WARM CONVERSATION WITH FRIENDS RATHER THAN A COMMERCIAL YOU BROADCAST TO FACELESS STRANGERS.

The results of this automated system have been staggering. It's allowed ministries to dream big, beyond what their staff could ever have done alone, calling on donors one by one. It's helped ministries reach deeper and wider into their donor file — shifting their mindset from growth by *addition* to growth by *multiplication*.

It ensures that the ongoing warm "conversation" with your estate gift prospects is actually happening — quarter by quarter, and year after year. And the automated system frees up ministry staff to spend their time thanking new estate gift donors, and reaching out to prospects who are expressing fresh interest.

Just to give you a picture of how this automated ongoing "conversation" works: one of our ministry partners recently showed us a stack of donor records. Those records tracked the movement of their estate gift prospects through mail-back correspondence.

AN AUTOMATED DONOR DIALOGUE MOVES ESTATE GIFT GROWTH FROM ADDITION TO MULTIPLICATION.

For example, in the first year one of the donors requested some introductory "faith and family" content. Then in year 2, the donor expressed interest, indicating they would consider a gift in their Will to this ministry. And then in year 3, the donor reported to the ministry that they had now included the ministry in their Will.

And the entire process — from awareness to interest to action — all happened through automated mail-back correspondence.

Q We're going to really focus this year on planned giving receipt inserts, postcards, and newsletter articles. Isn't that wonderful?

Maybe.

It's a noble idea, but this well-intentioned approach by itself, is kind of like buying a beautiful new car that's stuck in first gear. At first, you're overflowing with anticipation and excitement about your shiny new vehicle and the adventure ahead. But very quickly, the tingly feelings go away when you realize you're not going to get very far.

A newly hired development staff member of a large ministry enthusiastically described to me the variety of planned gift marketing communications she was going to create over the next 12 months: receipt inserts, postcards, donor testimonials, newsletter articles, website content, social media, and more.

"What do you hope these communications will accomplish?" I asked.

After a moment of silence, she acknowledged she hadn't really thought about that. Her job was to create an overall positive donor experience, and her belief was that creating and sending out a flurry of imaginative planned gift communications would somehow contribute to that.

Now, we do like consistent multi-channel messaging. In fact, it's the foundation of every successful and growing planned gift program we've ever observed or been a part of. But unleashing a whirlwind of planned gift communications with little or no concern for whether it's connecting with donors is another example of ineffective monologue marketing.

> UNLEASHING A WHIRLWIND OF PLANNED GIFT COMMUNICATIONS USUALLY RESULTS IN INEFFECTIVE MONOLOGUE MARKETING.

The development director's feelings of excitement had everything to do with her personal desire to work on new ideas, be creative, and design materials with original messaging and images. But she had very little interest in what fruit might result from this enormous effort she was about to undertake — quite surprising since we had estimated there was $250 million of estate gift potential in their existing donor file!

To avoid the fairly common temptation to crank out lots of creative planned gift communications with little or no concern for results, we recommend you first develop a compelling goal that you, your leadership and your team are excited about (more on that in the FAQ section of Chapter 5).

Secondly, build your communication strategy around the three predictable steps that every estate giver takes. If you

RIDE THE WAVE

understand this 3-step process, you will be well-positioned to ride the wave, seeing more estate gifts than ever as you minister to the hearts of your donors:

Step 1: Awareness. To open up donor dialogue, start talking about things *they* care about. That means instead of communicating what *you* care about (ex. ministry highlights, how to include us in your Will, etc.), think about the desires, needs, and fears your donor is experiencing and speak directly into those.

> BEGIN BY TALKING ABOUT THINGS THAT DONORS CARE ABOUT INSTEAD OF WHAT THE MINISTRY CARES ABOUT.

This is *so* important, because most of your donors have very busy and fulfilling lives, and simply getting their attention is a big deal. Their brain space is already maxed out on their marriages, kids, grandkids, home remodeling projects, next travel destination, church involvements, sports calendars, weekend and vacation plans.

I think it would be pretty safe to say that if you polled your board members and most faithful donors, *none* of them woke up this morning thinking about giving an estate gift to you. You need to *earn* the right to bring up that topic.

Most ministries bypass this crucial step and blitz their donors with well-intentioned planned giving receipt stuffers, newsletter articles and websites focused on *their* interests, but they unfortunately miss the mark with their intended audience.

Then after several months of dutifully delivering "awareness" messaging, with little or nothing to show for it, they conclude their donors aren't interested in planned giving, and give up. For some proven ideas and approaches on how to improve your front-end "awareness" messaging to donors, see Chapter 1 where I discuss drawing people in with inspiration over information.

Step 2: Interest. Once a donor has become *aware* of planned giving, the next step in the legacy gift dialogue is to find out if there is any *interest* in even considering a gift to your ministry in their Will. Unlike the first step ("awareness") where we are communicating a relevant message *to* the donor, the second step ("interest") is asking and listening for a response *from* the donor.

THE SECOND STEP IS ASKING AND LISTENING FOR A RESPONSE FROM THE DONOR.

This can happen in a variety of ways (ex. through the mail, online, at an event, through personal contact, and more). But this is honestly the step that most ministries miss — the ongoing process of *listening* to their donors. This is a major key to your overall success, so let me

DONOR DIALOGUE

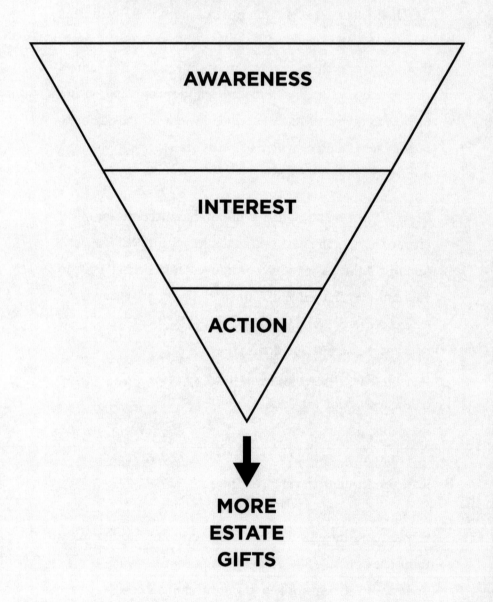

AWARENESS

INTEREST

ACTION

MORE
ESTATE
GIFTS

just urge you to really digest this game-changing dynamic. Please be aware that this step requires a little patience on your part.

Some donors will tell you they are interested right out of the gate. An immediate, positive response is encouraging and gives you an instant jolt of adrenaline. But for many of your eventual estate givers, it takes a few months or even years to get to that point.

That's because 99 percent of estate gifts are triggered by unpredictable life events such as changes in health, finances, family, etc. Your job then, is to keep the door open with your donors, earning the right to check in with them periodically as a trusted friend and ministry partner.

GENERATE INTEREST THROUGH AN ONGOING PROCESS OF LISTENING — THROUGH THE MAIL, ONLINE, AT EVENTS, AND IN PERSON.

Then when those unpredictable life events inevitably do happen, you are there, with an already-established relationship, ready to serve them in the third and final "action" step of their legacy journey.

Step 3: Action. This is the practical, how-to part of the dialogue that gives the donor the information they need to take their third and final step in the legacy journey.

There are two common pitfalls here you want to avoid. The first pitfall is that ministries sometimes just ignore this step all together. They aren't ready to serve donors who are ready to take action. They either don't know what to communicate, or they just assume their donors will figure it out on their own.

ENCOURAGE ACTION WITH EASY-TO-UNDERSTAND "NEXT STEP" INFORMATION FOR YOUR DONORS.

The second pitfall is that ministries skip past the *awareness* and *interest* steps and jump ahead into *action*, promoting content that explains how to make a bequest, an IRA rollover gift, a charitable gift annuity, etc.

But if no groundwork has been laid, and no interest has been expressed by the donor, it's like asking someone to marry you on the first date! You laugh, but this is actually very common.

The key to success is to first guide your donors into a dialogue that moves them from *awareness* to *interest* and then on to *action*. When your donor is ready to act, you simply want to be a trusted educational resource for them.

You do not need to be a planned giving "expert" or endorse a particular action step or solution. You just need to be ready with two or three good options to help them take their next step.

For example, perhaps you have an attorney on your board or a local community foundation. You can also contact a gift planning expert who specializes in this area, such as Barnabas Foundation, National Christian Foundation, Orchard Foundation, MB Foundation, and others. Or you can contact our team at Money for Ministry for some ideas to help get you started.

Q We tried a planned giving survey and it didn't work very well. How come?

A planned giving survey program is actually one of the best and most effective ways to engage interested estate gift prospects because it allows you to reach more people and achieve higher response rates. But for a planned giving survey to be successful, you'll want to think of it as one part of an ongoing dialogue, not a "one and done" monologue.

Here are four proven keys to using surveys effectively as a way to engage donors in an ongoing dialogue:

Follow up. The number one reason planned giving surveys fail is a lack of effective follow-up correspondence — whether by mail or personal contact. A survey may have generated lots of interest, but because there was no intention or plan in place to serve the ongoing interests of the donors, the development team just moved on to the next thing, and the interested donor prospects were left hanging.

Remember what I said earlier about how almost every estate gift is triggered by an unpredictable life event? Imagine your ministry sends out a planned giving survey, and hundreds or even thousands of people respond, but you aren't ready to take action yet.

If there is no follow-up system in place to maintain a mail-back dialogue over the next few months or even years, you have done a tremendous disservice to your donors and likely left millions of ministry dollars on the table. Expectations were raised with no way to fulfill them.

ONLY SEND A SURVEY IF YOU HAVE A SOLID 12-36 MONTH FOLLOW-UP SYSTEM IN PLACE TO SERVE INTERESTED DONORS.

We'd recommend that you *not* send a survey unless you have a solid 12-36 month follow-up system in place to serve interested donors. A survey is a great way to *begin* the dialogue, but a terrible way to *end* it.

Planned giving surveys are most effective if they are part of a recurring system that keeps the door of conversation open with engaged prospects. You can accomplish this by offering donors a variety of ways to stay engaged, such as mail-back correspondence, special events, and personal contact.

You could certainly take a shot at setting this up yourself in-house. But honestly, the ministries that have attempted keeping on top of who gets what and when, told us they loved the results, but hated all the work it created for their team. So our team at Money for Ministry spent nearly a year building a cost-effective, automated follow-up system that minimizes staff time and maximizes estate gift results. And we've been refining it ever since.

Language. We heard about a national charity that sent out 35,000 planned gift surveys and got *zero* responses — not even one! What happened? The language of the survey was all about what the donors can do for the organization when they die:

> *Would you like to include us in your will?*
> *Would you like an informational brochure about*
>   *planned giving?*
> *Would you like to talk to an adviser about your*
>   *estate plan?*

There was no attempt to understand or truly serve the donor. This organization came off like a vulture circling a wounded animal, waiting for the right moment to strike. Donors are threatened by this kind of approach, and want to run for their lives.

Approach. It's very tempting for ministry leaders to rely on email for their planned giving surveys. After all, it's pretty easy and inexpensive to send an email. There's nothing wrong with email surveys — and we certainly use and recommend this approach as part of an overall marketing mix — because they can help you dig deeper into your file of estate gift prospects.

EMAIL SURVEYS ALONE TEND TO DELIVER A LOWER QUALITY AND QUANTITY OF ESTATE GIFT PROSPECTS.

But email should *never* be used as your primary lead generation tool, no matter how cheap and easy it appears to be.

That's because we've found that email tends to deliver a lower *quality* and *quantity* of estate gift prospects. Add to that the reality that most organizations don't have accurate or up-to-date email addresses for large chunks of their donor files.

And even if they did, many of the donors who respond to planned gift survey emails are not necessarily your best estate gift prospects (ex. the loyal, longtime, older givers who prefer physical mail).

Another approach we like, but recommend you use cautiously, is the telephone survey. The results are pretty good because of the personal touch, but the cost to surface qualified prospects and new estate gifts is significantly higher than other more cost-effective approaches we recommend.

Audience. Another pretty common mistake we see ministries make with surveys is testing the approach with the wrong audience. There is a common misconception, for example, that the best estate gift prospects are your wealthy, older donors.

Expensive database analysis tools (from companies that don't specialize in planned giving) perpetuate this myth by giving disproportionate priority to donors that fit this profile.

So when a ministry who was using one of these tools asked us for help, we suggested first running a test using their high-priced analysis tool with a portion of their prospects, alongside our analysis with another portion of their prospect pool.

We did that, and their expensive analysis tool yielded a 4 percent response, while our approach yielded an 18 percent response — drawing from the same donor pool!

The difference was simple: we focused on longtime, frequent, and recent donors to begin the planned gift ministry conversation. The other company focused solely on wealthy older donors. I don't share this statistic to pat ourselves on the back, but rather to make the

> TEST YOUR SURVEY PROGRAM WITH LONGTIME, FREQUENT, AND RECENT DONORS REGARDLESS OF WEALTH OR AGE.

point that *how you segment* your planned gift prospects can have a massive impact on your opportunity to dialogue with your best estate gift prospects.

Q We got some pretty good results with our planned giving campaign. Can we move on to the next thing now?

Parents often joke (or complain) about their kids asking "are we there yet?" on a road trip.

My youngest son Lane is one of those kids. He frequently checks in to see how we are progressing toward our destination, so I made a deal with him. He can ask me one (and only one) question before our next stop. If he can do that, I'll buy him a snack when we get there. I'm happy to report that solved the problem!

CHRISTIAN NONPROFIT LEADERS WANT TO KNOW HOW TO MEASURE SUCCESS AND WHEN THEY'VE ARRIVED.

When it comes to their planned giving, Christian nonprofit leaders want to know, "are we there yet?" It's a fair question. They want to know how to measure success, and when they've *arrived*.

So here's the deal. You never actually "arrive" in planned giving. If you are at all interested in making the most of your donor file's estate gift potential, you'll want to see planned gift ministry as a journey not an event. A dialogue not a monologue.

Here are three keys to help you do that:

Duration. When ministry leaders ask me "how long should we keep doing this planned giving stuff?" I always smile and recommend what I call the "ULR" approach — Until the Lord Returns. That's because kingdom-impacting, planned gift ministry growth is a marathon, not a sprint.

> MAKE PLANNED GIFT MINISTRY A NATURAL ONGOING PART OF WHO YOU ARE AND EVERYTHING YOU DO.

Unlike a capital campaign, where you are raising a specific amount of money for a specific project by a specific deadline, a thriving planned gift ministry isn't something you do once and move on.

It becomes a natural part of who you are and everything you do. It becomes part of your ministry's DNA — a way you faithfully serve your donors and help them participate in an ultimate act of stewardship and worship.

Dialogue. A lot of ministries are really good at staying in touch with their *major* donors. They visit them, call them, and invite them to events on a regular basis. They intuitively understand that major gifts are cultivated through ongoing *dialogue* and relationship. Yet when it comes to estate gifts (which by the way *is* a major gift) many ministries do the opposite.

Instead of creating an ongoing dialogue with their estate gift prospects, they use a one-way monologue marketing approach. Instead of serving the interests of their donors, they look like they are "selling" planned giving.

ESTABLISH YOUR MINISTRY AS A TRUSTED FRIEND AND PARTNER IN THE LEGACY JOURNEY.

One of the largest ministries in the country, with a very successful planned gift ministry program, confirmed what we have seen thousands of times in the ministries we serve: the key to maximum long-term success in planned gift ministry is to establish yourself as a trusted friend and partner to your donors walking alongside them in their legacy journey. You do that by creating an engaging and ongoing dialogue — by mail, online, at events, and in person.

Depth. You can skim some pretty good estate gift results off the top with a one-time survey or campaign, but if you want your ministry to enjoy its *full* potential, you'll want to explore the depths of your donor file.

Every donor, volunteer, and prayer partner (no matter their demographics on paper) can quite easily include you in their Will, and therefore every one of them is an estate gift prospect.

Every ministry we've ever interacted with has millions (and in some cases billions) of estate gift potential within their existing donor database. As I pointed out earlier, it is not at all uncommon to see $50,000 estate gifts from the masses of donors who are giving $50 per year.

DEVELOP A PLAN THAT ENGAGES YOUR ENTIRE DONOR FILE OVER TIME IN THE PLANNED GIFT MINISTRY DIALOGUE.

To find these people, you want to look way beyond your assigned major givers. Even beyond your faithful *mid*-level donors. What you really want to do is develop a plan that engages your entire donor file over time in the planned gift ministry dialogue.

RECAP

HOW TO RIDE THE WAVE OF DIALOGUE OVER MONOLOGUE

Treat your planned gift messaging like a warm conversation with friends rather than a commercial you broadcast to faceless strangers.

Unleashing a whirlwind of planned gift communications with little or no concern for what they are actually accomplishing is ineffective monologue marketing.

Build awareness by speaking into the desires, needs, and fears your donor is experiencing.

Generate interest through an ongoing process of listening.

Encourage action with easy-to-understand "next step" information for your donors.

Only send a survey if you have a solid 12-36 month follow-up system in place to serve interested donors.

Use survey language that shows you are truly interested in people, their preferences, and their passions.

Email surveys alone tend to deliver a lower quality and quantity of estate gift prospects.

Test your survey program with longtime, frequent, and recent donors regardless of wealth or age.

Make planned gift ministry part of your organization's DNA — a natural ongoing part of who you are and everything you do.

Establish your ministry as a trusted friend and partner in the legacy journey.

Develop a plan that engages your entire donor file over time in the planned gift ministry dialogue.

WHAT'S WORKING
DONOR DIALOGUE

" Just as my own personal relationship with the Lord grows and deepens when I engage in a dialogue of prayer with Him, our family of legacy givers at Bethany Christian Services grows and deepens as we engage in prayerful dialogue with them. Our annual planned giving dialogue survey has increased to double digit response rates over the last two years. We believe this is a result of how we screen and filter our database, increasing the number of total surveys we send out, and increasing the number of "live" conversations we're now having with our donors all year long."

Bruce Hakim
Bethany Christian Services

"And if you say 'yes' to an estate gift today,
I'll etch your name on my dashboard."

3

THE WAVE OF SERVING OVER SELLING

Caring precedes commitment

Convincing my wife Beckie to marry me took a while. About two years, actually.

To be fair, Beckie had at least a couple of good reasons to hesitate, take her time, and decide if she *really* wanted to commit to me for the rest of her life.

First was the episode about me taking drugs for money. Now it's not as bad as it sounds. But when you're dating someone, perception is reality.

In my senior year of college, there was a three-week period between semesters where students could take elective classes or work. I was debating what I should do, until I saw an intriguing ad placed by a pharmaceutical company about an hour away.

They were experimenting with a new anti-anxiety drug, and were looking for 30 volunteers to live on site for two weeks while they administered the drug and monitored any side effects. I was secretly hoping for the hair loss study, but hey, beggars can't be choosers.

> I THINK TAKING DRUGS FOR MONEY MADE BECKIE QUESTION MY CREDENTIALS AS A PREACHER'S KID.

I probably should have been a little suspicious when I joined the room full of applicants, and realized I was the only college student among this fine group of ex-convicts and unemployed drifters. But the lure of earning $1,200 while eating like a king with three meals a day and hanging out in their well-equipped rec room was too much for this college student to pass up.

Looking back, I think it made Beckie (and her parents) question my "credentials" as a preacher's kid!

Then there was my van.

I thought it would be fun to check out an auto auction and see if I could find an affordable vehicle there. To my delight, there was a parking lot full of cars in my price range. But none of them stood out — except one.

It was an extra-long black van with a beautiful rainbow-colored stripe along the side. It featured red shag carpeting along the interior floor and walls, set off by red lighting around the perimeter of the ceiling, red padded chairs in the front and middle of the van, and even a small stove and sink in the back!

I was so proud of my purchase, I couldn't wait to show Beckie. I picked her up at a school event, and told her I had a big surprise waiting for her in the parking lot.

We walked out together, and I waved my arm toward the van like an emcee introducing the featured entertainment for the night. With great fanfare, I asked "Well, what do you think of my new vehicle?"

Thinking I was pointing to the shiny new Cutlass Supreme sedan parked directly next to my van, her eyes lit up and she praised me for my excellent taste in cars. When I could see she was aiming her approving glances at the wrong vehicle, I sheepishly redirected her attention to the large black beast occupying one and a half parking spaces right next to it.

HER WORST FEARS CONFIRMED, SHE SMILED AND ASKED, "WHERE DID YOU GET THE VAN?

She studied my face carefully to see if I was joking. Her worst fears confirmed, she flashed a polite smile, and awkwardly asked "where did you get it?"

"An auto auction," I replied. "Would you like to take a test drive together?"

"How about if I just sit in it for now," she offered. "I need to get back and finish some homework."

Translation: Beckie wasn't "sold" on the van, and I was starting to wonder if she was ever going to be "sold" on me.

I needed a new approach. I wanted to marry her, but was pretty sure she still had some reasonable doubts about me. So I decided I needed to slow down and "serve" her rather than trying to "sell" her on the idea of marrying me.

EARNING THE AFFECTION AND TRUST OF YOUR DONORS OVER TIME OPENS THE DOOR FOR LIFETIME ESTATE GIFT COMMITMENTS.

So I made compilation recordings of her favorite music. I wrote sappy love songs for her on my guitar. I made her laugh as we did things she enjoyed like playing games or working on puzzles. I organized a missions trip to Haiti with her and some friends. I took her to places she loved, like this little creek where we would do devotions together and where I eventually proposed to her.

Over time, God was weaving our hearts and lives together, and on October 2, 1993 my dad married us in front of a few hundred family and friends. Looking back, it was a very gradual process for me to earn Beckie's trust and affection.

Estate gifts come to Christian nonprofits in the exact same way. Gradually earning the trust and affection of your donors over time opens the door for lifetime estate gift commitments. But this means letting go of the tendency to want to "sell" an estate gift, and replacing it with a desire to *serve* your donors.

This "serving" looks like helping your donors 'get their house in order' so they can avoid the headache and hassle of *not* having an estate plan. It comes from a sincere desire to see their family experience the joy of good communication with each other, and make an eternal impact for generations to come.

But sadly, this is often *not* how it plays out for many ministries. Some development directors — feeling pressure to hit this year's budget goal from their boards and bosses — prefer to skip past the "serving" part and instead try to "sell" estate gifts. They focus their planned gift marketing communications on the *transaction* instead of the *relationship*. Selling instead of serving.

Instead of trying to understand the needs and desires of their audience, and helping them discover the legacy they want to leave for their kids, grandkids and the ministries they love, they lead off with "marriage proposal" questions like:

Want to speak to our planned giving expert?
May we send you our estate planning booklet?
Are we in your Will?

For your donors, this all sounds like asking for marriage on the first date. People feel sold to instead of served. That approach doesn't work in dating, and it doesn't work in the development office either.

FREQUENTLY ASKED QUESTIONS

Q **Should we partner with a gift planning organization such as National Christian Foundation, Barnabas Foundation, Orchard Foundation, PhilanthroCorp, MB Foundation, etc.?**

The organizations you're considering are the best in the business. We know them well, have collaborated with all of them, and have nothing but the highest praise for their reputations, excellent work, and the contributions they've made to advancing the cause of Christ.

The great strength these organizations bring to Christian nonprofits is the ability to help donors execute planned gifts. They have all helped numerous ministry-minded donors give away millions of dollars to the cause of Christ through smart planning. In other words, when your donors are ready to take action, these expert Christian gift planners are ready and able to serve them well.

The key phrase in that last paragraph was "when your donors are *ready* to take action." Our gift planning friends don't know when your donors are ready to take action until *you* tell them a donor needs help and is open to having a conversation. And the best way for you to know who is interested and needs help is by creating a system of ongoing dialogue with your donors (see Chapter 2).

On any given day, only a fraction of your donor file is ready to take action on a planned gift. But as I noted in Chapter 2, there are two important steps that lead your donors to take action: awareness and interest.

So before you call in a gift planner to serve the donors that need help finalizing a gift, you need to first *surface* some donor interest. And you do that by building a consistent mail-back dialogue with your donors, building a relationship of trust with them. Then when their unexpected life event happens, and they're ready to create or update their Will, they'll think of you first.

> YOU NEED TO "SURFACE" DONOR INTEREST BEFORE ANYONE CAN "SERVE" THE DONOR'S DESIRE TO TAKE ACTION.

Again, if you need help creating this dialogue, please let our team know. Our specialty is helping ministries *surface* new estate gift donors and interested prospects. Then get ready. Some of those *surfaced* estate gift donors and interest prospects will need to be *served*.

They may not have a local attorney, or want to use an online Will-creation site. Or they may have a complex estate, family situation, or business. That's where the gift planning experts come in.

To sum it up: it's surface then serve.

Let me take a minute to unpack the differences between "surfacing" and "serving," because if you understand this nuance, you will be well on your way to riding the wave to more estate gifts than you ever thought possible.

When we talk about "surfacing" donors, we mean that your job is to manage the front-end "dating" relationship. Develop an ongoing dialogue with your donors that builds genuine love and rapport.

This comes from showing an interest in them as people, and demonstrating that you care about their unique passions and preferences. Give them ample opportunities to express their interest along the way through interactive mailings, websites, emails, events, and personal contacts.

> SURFACING YOUR ESTATE GIFT PROSPECTS IS THE ART OF "DATING" THEM, BUILDING GENUINE LOVE AND RAPPORT.

And then how do you *serve* donors who express interest and are ready to take action? For most estate gift donors, *you* don't need to do anything. They aren't expecting you or any charity to help them take action. They are what we call the "self-serve" donors. And there are a *lot* of them.

When they're ready to take action on a planned gift, they already have a solution in mind. It might be an attorney from their local church or parish. It might be an online Wills site

SURFACE

MORE
ESTATE
GIFTS

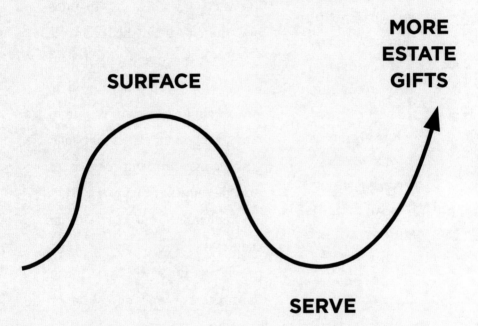

SERVE

like LegalZoom or USLegalForms. Millions of people go this route, and you should be very happy about that.

They think you're great at what you do, but most wouldn't necessarily think of you when they want to move ahead with estate planning. And that's totally normal and fine.

> WHEN THE DONOR IS READY TO TAKE ACTION, AND NEEDS HELP, YOU'LL WANT TO HAVE SOME RESOURCES READY, SUCH AS AN EXPERT CHRISTIAN GIFT PLANNER.

But there are others who may ask where to get help. In situations like these, where the donor is ready to take action but needs help and doesn't know where to turn, you'll want to have some resources ready, such as an expert Christian gift planner in your corner to provide some back-end support.

Remember our caution in chapter 1 about not scaring people away with "too much information?" Well, once a donor has expressed interest and is ready to take action, that caution goes away. Now is the time to connect them with the expert advice they need.

Q Should we hire a planned giving person on our team?

There are some very good reasons to consider hiring a planned giving officer for your team. For larger ministries, it's often a necessity to have a person or even a full team directing the planned gift program. And in some cases, it makes sense for smaller organizations to have someone internally who can provide a higher level of coordination, continuity, and contact with donors.

But there have also been a number of occasions where ministries call and ask us if they should hire a planned giving person, and for that particular ministry we've recommended *against* it, or at least have advised they use caution. And the reason is because there are three potential risks in bringing on dedicated planned giving staff without careful consideration:

Risk #1: Scaring Your Donors. If your job is to call donors and introduce yourself as "Joe the planned giving rep" or "Sally the estate gift specialist," that can have the unintended consequence of scaring or confusing your donors before you can get the first sentence out.

Most donors don't know what "planned giving" means, so you'll want to avoid phrases like that which confuse donors. And anything with "estate gift" in the title can give donors the impression you're going to come in and ask for "marriage" on the first date. Instead we recommend that you choose a job title that is donor-friendly such as Donor Advisor or Ministry Representative.

Risk #2: Boring Your Donors. Remember what we said in Chapter 1 about ministries wanting to give their donors way too much information about planned giving? That risk is especially true for Christian nonprofits who hire planned giving specialists.

TRAINED PLANNED GIVING REPS ARE HAPPY TO SHARE THEIR VAST KNOWLEDGE WITH YOUR DONORS.

These wonderful professionals have been trained, they attend conferences, and are technical experts in the details of how every planned gift tool and technique works. And they'd be happy to share their vast ocean of knowledge with you, your donors, or anyone who will listen.

The problem with this approach, as we noted earlier, is that most of your donors need inspiration before they need information. Ironically, some of the most effective reps we've worked with have had little or no planned giving background.

So whether you hire an expert, or someone who is newer to the field, we recommend you recruit interesting, winsome, relational people — with just enough basic planned giving knowledge to be helpful.

Risk #3: Limited Results. When ministries hire a planned giving officer, they generally assign them a caseload of say 100-200 donors and prospects to serve. The first concern here is that even in a good year, a very ambitious and outgoing donor rep can only reach a very tiny sliver of your overall donor file. In all likelihood, those donors will be served very well.

But that means you still have thousands of donors who are left unserved, and millions of dollars are inadvertently left on the table, despite a ministry's best intentions.

It's very important then, for your ministry to have a plan to reach beyond its relatively small list of assigned donors and go deep into the masses of unassigned prospects. (For more on how to do this effectively, see our recommended 3-step process in Chapter 2).

For optimal estate gift growth, teamwork makes the dream work. So if and when you add planned giving staff, be careful not to unintentionally create another silo internally. Planned giving? Oh, that's so-and-so's job.

> FOR OPTIMAL ESTATE GIFT GROWTH, TEAMWORK MAKES THE DREAM WORK.

In virtually every effective planned gift program we've been a part of, the ministry took a team-based approach. In many cases, those organizations didn't necessarily have *anyone* assigned full-time to planned giving.

Rather, it was the development director casting a vision to everyone on the development and marketing teams that planned giving is a huge priority.

The message goes something like this: "From now on, we *all* will share in the success and growth of our program. That means integration with our receipts, direct mail program, newsletters, website, event strategy, and our existing personal donor contacts."

The team-based approach is a very powerful one because now you're engaging *all* of your team in the work they are already doing, and leveraging it for much greater impact.

> THE TEAM APPROACH IS POWERFUL BECAUSE IT LEVERAGES WHAT YOU'RE ALREADY DOING.

The person who coordinates your direct mail appeals, for example, keeps doing what they're doing. But now instead of just fishing for $50 checks, they are also now surfacing $50,000 estate gift prospects. See the difference?

The team-based approach also improves your engagement with all of your donors. You're no longer limited to a list of 100 or 200 selected planned gift prospects. Now you can serve your *entire donor file* the way they want to be served.

They're already telling you *how* they like to engage with you. Some only respond to your mailings. Others prefer to go online. Still others would rather just go to your events. And some are used to you reaching out to them in person.

The team-based approach allows you to *integrate* the estate gift message naturally and seamlessly across all communication channels, to all donors, significantly maximizing your estate gift growth potential.

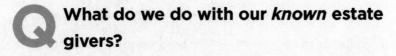 What do we do with our *known* estate givers?

I LOVE this question because it usually means the ministry leader has the kind of heart and mindset it takes to really *thrive* with estate gifts.

You would not *believe* (or maybe you would!) how often we interact with ministries that have done *nothing* with their known estate givers. Some may have sent a generic thank you letter, then moved on.

Or occasionally we'll get a call from a new development director who will come across an old file drawer full of estate gift notifications from over 10 years ago. And they'll call us and ask, "Should we do something with these?"

> **ESTATE GIVERS ARE COMMITTING A PORTION OF THEIR LIVES OF HARD WORK AND SAVINGS TO YOU.**

The simple answer is "Yes! You should do *something* with your known estate givers." Their estate gift means they are committing a portion of their net worth to your ministry. It's probably the result of a lifetime of hard work, and maybe some estate planning, and some prayer. And it's likely the largest gift they will ever make!

They have been faithful friends of your ministry for years. If you acknowledge and thank your estate givers for their extraordinary gift, and build relationships with them, God will be glorified. Your ministry will also continue to grow, because nurtured estate givers tend to give much more — both now and later.

TREAT YOUR ESTATE GIVERS LIKE MAJOR DONORS-BECAUSE THEY ARE.

So then back to the original question: what exactly should you do with known estate givers? I'll start with the simple answer: *treat them like a major donor.*

How do you that? Well, if someone called you today and pledged $50,000 to your ministry, what would you do? Whatever you would do for a person who gives you a big gift *today*, do the same for the person who is giving you a big gift *tomorrow*.

For example, if you knew in advance that a donor was considering a gift of $50,000 or $100,000 to your ministry in their Will, you'd probably agree it might be worth sending them an occasional note, making a periodic phone call, or dropping in sometime for a visit, right?

Every donor is different, so there's no cookie cutter formula for how best to treat your known estate givers, but here are some approaches that ministries we work with are using very effectively:

Legacy Society Newsletter. Create a semi-annual newsletter written specifically for your known legacy givers. Let them know how much you appreciate them.

Give them content unique to them that they would find valuable (ex. a note and headshot from you to build the personal connection, an article about how to update an estate plan, advice on how to communicate estate gifts to adult children, etc.)

Some ministries object to the phrase "Legacy Society" and others like it. That's okay. It doesn't matter what you call it, but it *does* matter that you communicate with them.

> LET YOUR ESTATE GIVERS KNOW HOW MUCH YOU APPRECIATE THEM WITH SPECIAL COMMUNICATIONS AND EVENTS.

Special Events. Ministries get really creative with this one. We work with ministries that have hosted art exhibits, trips to the zoo, thank you luncheons, visits to botanical gardens, and more. The point is to create an event that your legacy givers (and interested prospects) would want to come to.

This means you're not "selling" anything (they're already sold on your ministry and the concept of estate gifts), you're simply communicating your gratitude in a way that nurtures the relationship. What legacy givers want is a place to belong and be affirmed. They want an opportunity to build on the relationship and deepen their commitment to your organization.

Personal Contacts. If you're currently cultivating relationships with major and mid-level donors, then you already know *how* to do this. But I want to challenge you to rethink *who* you do this with.

IF YOU KNOW "HOW" TO TREAT MAJOR DONORS, IT'S TIME TO RETHINK "WHO" GETS THAT TREATMENT.

Most ministries will say something like "We call and thank every donor who gives a gift above $500," and that's wonderful. But what about the 83 year-old widow who has been giving you $5 per month for the past 20 years?

She is an *excellent* candidate for a $50,000 estate gift, but if no one is even acknowledging her, let alone thanking her for her $5 gifts, or sending her birthday and Christmas cards, she may decide to direct her "gift of a lifetime" elsewhere.

RECAP

HOW TO RIDE THE WAVE OF SERVING OVER SELLING

If you earn your donors' affection and trust over time, some will eventually commit the gift of a lifetime to you — a charitable gift in their Will.

You need to "surface" donor interest before anyone can "serve" their desire to take action.

When the donor is ready to take action, and needs help, you'll want to have some resources ready, such as an expert Christian gift planner.

Choose a job title that is donor-friendly such as Donor Advisor or Ministry Representative.

Hire interesting, winsome, relational people — with just enough planned giving knowledge to be helpful.

Reach beyond your relatively small list of assigned donors to go deep into the masses of your unassigned prospects.

For optimal estate gift growth, teamwork makes the dream work.

Treat your known estate givers like major donors (regardless of their current gift size).

WHAT'S WORKING
TEAMWORK

" When a ministry only has one or two people who focus on planned giving, it is hard to have a culture that truly embraces the importance of it. Developing a team approach means more staff see how important it is to the ministry's long-term sustainability. And as staff understand how estate planning is actually a ministry to donors, it allows new opportunities to engage with givers because staff look for ways to include a planned giving component in events, mailings, campaigns, etc. That relieves the burden of only one person trying to constantly give planned giving the attention it deserves."

Elaine Watkins
Precept Ministries International

The "widow's mite" donor felt strangely
out of place at the major donor reception.

4

THE WAVE OF WIDOWS OVER THE WEALTHY

**Your smallest donors are often
your biggest opportunities**

Why does God make such a *big* deal out of *little* things? I mean, just look at the Bible and our faith experience — it's FULL of *little* people and *little* things making a *huge* difference!

Like the little shepherd boy named David taking down the giant Goliath.

The "little town of Bethlehem" where Jesus the Savior of the world was born.

The little bit of bread and fish brought by a little boy that fed the huge crowd.

The tiny, little mustard seed Jesus used to illustrate what it takes to have great, mountain-moving faith.

Zacchaeus the "wee little man" whose great sin was overcome with even greater forgiveness and repentance.

Songs we sang as kids like "This Little Light of Mine" and "It Only Takes a Spark."

The anticipation of hearing Jesus say one day, "Well done, good and faithful servant. You have been faithful over a little, I will set you over much."

It's absolutely incredible to think about how our big and awesome God, the Creator and Sustainer of the universe, went to such great lengths to show us how much He values *little* things and seemingly insignificant people.

Jesus amplified this surprising pattern by redefining what we all refer to in ministry fundraising today as a "major donor." When He wanted to illustrate what *really* big giving looks like, He didn't gather his rich friends for a lavish major donor weekend event at a 5-star resort on the shores of Galilee. And He didn't do a wealth screen of high-capacity donor prospects in Jerusalem.

Instead, He shocked everyone by pointing out a little old lady hobbling forward with two little coins in her hand, giving all she had to express her love for God, seemingly unnoticed, as a humble act of worship.

And now here we are, over 2,000 years later, and most ministries are looking past the "little" widow's mite donors that Jesus redefined as major donors. These faithful friends never get mentioned when ministries strategize who they need to see for their year-end and capital campaign calls. They never make the headlines in the philanthropy materials we read. And they never get featured in the numerous major donor fundraising workshops and webinars we attend.

But they are quietly and humbly triggering a revolution in generosity, fueling the largest generational wealth transfer in history.

These masses of "hidden major donors" are faithfully (and often sacrificially) giving $10 per month or maybe $100 per year. No one on your development team knows who they are.

> MOST MINISTRIES ARE LOOKING PAST THE FACELESS, FAITHFUL "WIDOW'S MITE DONORS" THAT JESUS REDEFINED AS MAJOR DONORS.

Yet these faceless, faithful givers are often able and willing to leave estate gifts of $50,000 or $100,000 or in some cases much more, not because they are hoping to be featured in your newsletter or recognized at your next public event, but rather because they are so grateful to God for His faithfulness to them over the years.

They've enjoyed God's presence in their lives, their families, their churches, and a lifetime of blessing, and now through their estate, they want to return an offering of thanks to God, their ultimate act of worship.

I'll never forget when we began working with a wonderful, nationally-recognized ministry to children and families. One of the first things I asked them to do was generate a list of every donor they had on file who had already notified them of a future estate gift. I passed out the report to the development team, and a stunned silence fell across that little conference room.

> MANY ESTATE GIVERS WANT TO RETURN AN OFFERING OF THANKS TO GOD AS THEIR ULTIMATE ACT OF WORSHIP.

There they were, looking at the names of a couple hundred longtime, faithful donors to their ministry, all of whom had committed to an estate gift — the list was worth many millions of dollars to their worthy cause. But you could almost see their jaws hit the table when they realized that, with few exceptions, they didn't know these people!

And right there, my friends, is a picture of what may be your greatest opportunity (and challenge) in the growth of your ministry: discovering and engaging your masses of widow's mite donors.

But I have some very good news to encourage you! They're already in your database. They already love you. And they have proven over and over again to the ministries we serve that they want to build a relationship with you.

The journey begins by seeing your countless "little" donors the way God sees them — as people, with names, that most others ignore. He's just waiting to surprise the world, yet again, with a powerful demonstration of how the little things that everyone else looks past can be used to accomplish great things, and make a big impact that will resonate for eternity.

FREQUENTLY ASKED QUESTIONS

So are all of our older, smaller donors good estate gift prospects?

Every donor — big or small — along with every volunteer and prayer partner in your database are estate gift prospects. That's because literally anyone on your list could decide to include you in their Will.

But when ministries ask us this question, what they really want to know is who are our *best* estate gift prospects? Their gut tells them their older, wealthier donors are their best prospects.

In fact, when ministries reach out to us to ask about planned gift marketing, one of the first things they often say is "We have an aging donor file, so we figured now is the time to get going on planned giving."

So yes, it's true that your older, smaller donors make up a large percentage of your best estate gift prospects. And if you simply focused your planned gift ministry outreach on your "widow's mite" donors, I think you'd find that to be a very fruitful and fulfilling experience.

But if your aim is to identify as many of your likely estate gift prospects as possible, Money for Ministry recommends beginning by filtering your donor file based on five predictors of likely estate gift donors:

Frequency. Donors who give to you on a regular basis are excellent estate gift prospects. This is especially true for monthly donors, but faithful once-a-year annual givers qualify as well. And that makes sense, right? These folks are thinking about you often, and care enough to go a step further and consistently support your ministry with their dollars.

Now think about that in terms of how Jesus said "where your treasure is there your heart will be also." That means your frequent donors are very much in love with you!

History. Estate gift donors also tend to have a very long history with your ministry. Their first gift to you may have come 15 or even 20 years ago. And it doesn't always have to be even that far back. We've found that for some Christian nonprofits, going back

> DONORS WHO HAVE GIVEN FREQUENTLY OVER TIME CAN BE SOME OF YOUR BEST ESTATE GIFT PROSPECTS.

even seven years produces a pool of donors who are familiar and connected enough to the ministry that they are now willing to consider an estate gift. Keep in mind that longtime donors like this tend to be older, but not necessarily.

Recency. We've found that donors who have made a gift sometime in the past 12-24 months, especially through the mail, are also fantastic prospects. Not only have they given you money recently to express their love and commitment, but because their gift came through the mail, we also know they are responsive to the number one donor communication channel of choice among estate gift donors.

Participation. Another clue that someone is likely to consider an estate gift is their personal participation in your ministry. They may have no giving history with you at all. Volunteers for example, have proven to be excellent estate gift prospects.

> VOLUNTEERS AND PRAYER PARTNERS ARE COMMITTED TO YOUR CAUSE AND CAN BE VERY OPEN TO CONSIDERING YOU IN THEIR WILL.

Why? Just like faithful donors of money, faithful donors of time have also demonstrated a deep passion and commitment to your worthy cause. And so a gift in the Will allows your volunteers, board members, prayer partners, etc. an opportunity to extend the impact of the investment they've made to you for generations to come.

Planning. Have you received any "donor advised fund" gifts lately, where donors send you checks through an investment company like Fidelity, or a gift planning organization like National Christian Foundation? This method of giving is rapidly growing in popularity because donors enjoy the convenience, simplicity, and flexibility.

And you should love these gifts too, not only for the immediate cash they provide your ministry, but also because they expand your pool of likely estate gift prospects.

That's because donor advised fund givers look a lot like estate givers — people who plan their giving, and are thinking beyond their checkbooks. In short, these thoughtful donors are "hot" estate gift prospects.

Q What about our lapsed donors?

I mentioned above that your recent mail-back donors can be some of your best estate gift prospects. But we would also encourage you to not overlook your lapsed donors, individuals you may not have heard from in a long time.

Many of your lapsed donors were faithful givers for many years, but because of changes in their health or finances, their giving to your ministry slowed down or even stopped . . . but they still love you. Their heart is still with you, they're just not able to give like they used to.

Many ministries would in-turn stop communicating with their previously-faithful lapsed donors. But what *should* you do? We recommend three things to help you optimize your estate gift potential with faithful-turned-lapsed donors:

Understand Them. We've found that lapsed donors are among the most misunderstood group in ministry donor files. Many Christian nonprofits assume that if a donor stops giving, they probably lost interest in the ministry, and are therefore no longer worth the cost of printing and postage to reconnect with them.

What's actually happening for many of your faithful "widow's mite" donors is that while their *current* giving has cooled down, their *future* giving is heating up! They are often making final revisions to their Will.

PAY ATTENTION TO LAPSED DONORS WHOSE CURRENT GIVING MAY BE COOLING DOWN WHILE THEIR FUTURE GIVING MAY BE HEATING UP.

These revisions will likely include estates gifts, which are often much larger than all of their *lifetime gifts combined* for any given ministry on their list of favorite charities. It's not uncommon, for example, for a "widow's mite" donor to give $250 per year for 20 years to a ministry — which is $5,000 in lifetime gifts. Then an estate gift for $50,000 comes in from that same donor — that's *10 times more* than that person ever gave over the course of their entire lifetime!

And who are these disproportionally large estate gifts going to? The ministries that remain friendly to these faithful-turned-lapsed donors, even when their giving slows down or stops. I call this the "bridal party effect."

When people get married, they choose groomsmen and bridesmaids based on their current group of friends. The same is true with estate givers. When they reach their late 70s or early 80s and decide it's time to make the final updates to their estate plan, they look at the list of ministries they've supported over the years, and assess who their current group of friends are.

> WHEN DONORS ARE MAKING FINAL WILL REVISIONS, THEY ASSESS WHO THEIR CURRENT MINISTRY FRIENDS ARE.

If you've been ignoring them because they landed on your lapsed donor list, you probably missed out on the largest gift they will ever give.

Love Them. Once you've identified your lapsed donors who have longtime faithful giving histories, the next step is to decide *how* you will love them.

For starters, that probably means having a conversation with your team and maybe even your direct-mail agency to ensure that these donors will never be ignored. The stakes are just too high. If these faithful supporters are no longer responding to your mail appeals, you might start by making sure they are receiving your newsletter or magazine updates.

The other thing to keep in mind, as we discussed in the previous chapter, is to treat your faithful, longtime "widow's mite" donors as though they are "major donors."

And if you make it a priority to love on these faithful friends, reaching out to them, and inviting them to events, you'll find (as many other ministries have found), that many wonderful doors begin to open for you.

Test Them. This is a very delicate time of life for your lapsed "widow's mite" donors. They have very likely experienced significant change in their lives. They may have lost a spouse they were married to for over 50 years. They may have moved out of the home where they raised their children and into a senior care facility. They are probably facing a number of health challenges. And they are very likely living on a fixed income with some anxiety about outliving their savings.

> WHEN YOU PRIORITIZE LOVING ON YOUR FAITHFUL DONOR FRIENDS, MANY WONDERFUL DOORS BEGIN TO OPEN FOR YOU.

All that to say, there may be some who are reluctant or even uninterested in corresponding with your ministry about estate gifts.

On the other hand, don't assume they are not interested because of all the changes that are happening in their lives.

Instead, see this as a tremendous opportunity to serve them and bless them at a time when they most need some peace of mind.

Test a few different approaches to see if there is any interest in estate planning. You might try a receipt insert with an offer that helps them leave a legacy for their families and the ministries they love. You might try a donor survey to see if they're open to having a dialogue with you. You might try a phone call or personal visit to discover ways you can pray for them and potentially help with their legacy planning.

Q Why do you call our smaller faithful givers "hidden major donors"?

The sheer quantity of faithful under the radar "widow's mite" donors should be a clue that this group is a big deal and you should be paying careful attention to them. In our experience, it would not be unusual for a thriving estate gift program to see 85 percent of their gifts come from these quiet, unassuming donors who don't appear on anyone's contact list.

But most ministry leaders don't see this. They may realize this group is faithfully sending in checks for $10 per month, and appreciate how these consistent gifts make their daily operations possible, but they rarely consider the enormous game-changing potential *behind* those gifts. They have a

DONOR PYRAMID

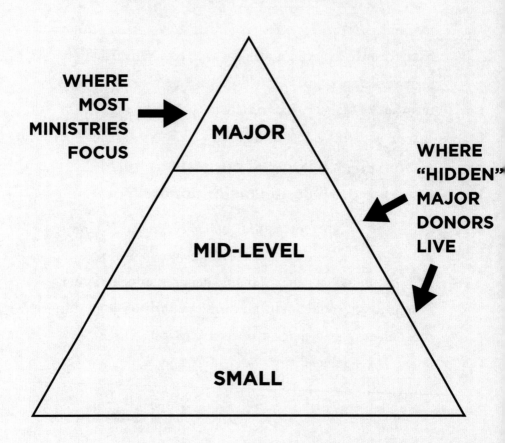

WHERE
MOST
MINISTRIES
FOCUS

MAJOR

WHERE
"HIDDEN"
MAJOR
DONORS
LIVE

MID-LEVEL

SMALL

huge pool of hidden major donors right under their noses and don't even realize it!

So can I let you in on a secret most ministries are missing? In addition to the ongoing stream of little checks you see coming in month after month, there are actually four kinds of *major gifts* that your under the radar "widow's mite" donors can bless and surprise you with. Here they are:

Estate Gifts. OK, this is the obvious one because it's the major theme of this book. But let's just take a moment to let this incredible reality sink in: behind every gift of $50 you receive is the possibility of a *$50,000* estate gift.

> BEHIND EVERY $50 GIFT IS THE POSSIBILITY OF A $50,000 ESTATE GIFT.

Do you have some $50 donors in your file? Of course you do! Probably lots of them. Have you ever thought of them as *major* gift prospects? If not, let me encourage you to decide that *now* is the time to start. Yes, some of these gifts will come years down the road. But if you have donors in their 80s and 90s, some of these estate gifts are just around the corner.

Major Gifts. Have you ever heard of an "acceleration gift?" In some cases, donors decide to *accelerate* their estate gift — which means they give it to you *now* while they're living, rather than after they are gone.

There are lots of reasons why someone would do this. Sometimes they're inspired by a compelling capital campaign they want to invest in. Other times it could be a known debt reduction need and they have a passion to see the ministry start fresh on strong financial footing. Or perhaps donors simply realize they have ample financial resources, and in the words of Christian financial counselor Ron Blue, want to "do their give'n while they're live'n so they are know'n where it's go'n."

> **ESTATE GIFT DONORS ARE OFTEN ABLE TO GIVE MUCH MORE NOW–NOT JUST LATER.**

Current Gifts. It's not unusual for estate givers to increase their current giving to operations. There is some research to suggest that donors who include a charity in their Will give *twice as much* to current operations.

We've seen this dynamic play out multiple times with ministries we serve. In fact, we've seen Christian nonprofits not only make a point to *discover* who their estate givers are, but then to intentionally *nurture* those relationships. And it seems to be making a big difference!

In one case, estate gift donors who were identified and cultivated gave 5 times more than the average giver on file. We currently work with a seminary where the robust and growing list of estate givers now give 12 times more than the average donor.

Asset Gifts. About 10 percent of your donor's wealth is in spendable cash. It's in their checkbooks. And when they give to you, they are most often contributing from their 10 percent pocket. But did you know that about 90 percent of your donors' wealth is in other assets — such as their home, their life insurance, their retirement savings, their property, and other investments?

Now I realize that cash is an "asset," so don't get all nerdy and technical on me here. I'm just making the point that your $10 per month "widow's mite" donors are sending those little checks from their 10 percent cash pocket.

But behind those checks is an enormous 90 percent pool of assets that they can give to you as well. We're talking *major* gifts, *now*. It could be from appreciated stock, or retirement savings, or the sale of a cottage or business or artwork. The possibilities are endless and honestly pretty staggering.

RECAP

HOW TO RIDE THE WAVE OF WIDOWS OVER THE WEALTHY

Most ministries are looking past the faceless, faithful "widow's mite" donors that Jesus redefined as major donors.

Run a list of frequent donors that have given you 100 gifts or more.

Run a report of donors that made their first gift to you 15 years ago or more.

Review your list of donors who gave any gift through the mail in the past 12 months.

Identify people who faithfully volunteer their time or pray for your ministry.

Ask your finance office for a list of donor advised fund donors from the past 36 months.

Identify your lapsed donors with longtime faithful giving histories.

Begin treating your faithful "widow's mite" donors as though they are major donors.

Test a few different approaches with lapsed "widow's mite" donors to see who might be interested in legacy planning.

See and treat your living estate givers as major donors regardless of their current gift size.

Challenge your estate givers to consider an "acceleration" gift.

Track the current giving from your estate givers while building the relationship with them.

Explore "asset gift" options with the estate givers you have an established relationship with.

WHAT'S WORKING
ENGAGING WIDOW'S MITE DONORS

" There isn't a gift that is more honoring, more encouraging, or more humbling to receive than that of the widow's mite. It reveals the heart of Jesus as it reminds me of what's truly of value to Him. We've been pleasantly surprised and very blessed to be a benefactor of estate gifts from these generous donors. It's surprising because historically, the amount of their gifts was very modest, and you would never have imagined, judging a book by its cover, they had the resources to provide such a generous gift."

Ed Tolsma
The Potter's House

Cathy missed the majestic mountain view
when a little molehill caught her eye.

(5)

THE WAVE OF MOUNTAINS OVER MOLEHILLS

Today's budget needs are smaller than tomorrow's huge potential

've seen some pretty amazing mountain views in my life, and maybe you have too.

I remember riding through Washington state on a visit to see my mom's side of the family as a kid. Mount St. Helens had recently erupted, triggering a massive record-setting collapse of the northern face of the mountain, and sending an ash cloud as far as 145 miles away.

My grandpa drove us around in his little Jayco RV, and I can still picture us pulling off to the side of the road so we could collect a little bit of ash as a souvenir (and yes, you can still buy little vials of that ash online for $20 — tell them I sent you.)

On our tenth wedding anniversary, Beckie and I drove through the beautiful, billboard-free Blue Ridge Mountains in North Carolina. One of the highlights was visiting Grandfather Mountain, named by pioneers who recognized the face of an old man in one of the cliffs.

The Samaritan's Purse headquarters was only 15 miles away, so we decided to stop by for a visit. We quickly learned that what looks like a "short" drive on a map can actually be a pretty "long" drive if it involves lots of hairpin turns through the mountains.

WHAT LOOKS LIKE A SHORT DRIVE ON A MAP CAN BE A LONG DRIVE IF IT INVOLVES LOTS OF HAIRPIN TURNS.

We eventually reached our destination, and were greeted warmly by Samaritan's Purse staff who had recruited us a few years earlier to be their first "Heart Project" family. This experience opened the door for us to host a baby from Mongolia who needed major heart surgery, along with her mother and an interpreter.

Our queasiness from the winding mountain drive quickly subsided as we praised the Lord together in the lobby for the good report and pictures they had received that same morning from the mountains of Mongolia.

Then one more "mountain memory" for now to help set the stage for the message of this chapter. I was traveling with two businessmen and two missionaries on a trip to Ecuador, organized by my former employer, Partners Worldwide. We were driving out of the capital city of Quito on our way to a small village, near the area where missionary martyrs Jim Elliott and Nate Saint had been killed 43 years earlier.

The beauty of the mountains against the backdrop of the purest blue sky I had ever seen was breathtaking. But that beauty came to a sudden halt when the driver of our jeep drove us across a deep valley, driving slowly on a swaying bridge made of ropes and rickety old beams of wood. I can't remember a time when my prayer life with Jesus felt so rich and passionate!

In all three of these mountain-top experiences, I took pictures and showed them to anyone who was interested, or even pretended to be interested. As you know, pictures never do justice to that kind of incredible scenery, but people could at least get a sense of the magnitude of Mount St. Helen, the autumn beauty surrounding Grandfather Mountain, and the lofty mountain grandeur in Ecuador.

> THE BEAUTY OF THE MOUNTAINS CAME TO A SUDDEN HALT WHEN OUR JEEP DROVE ACROSS A SWAYING ROPE BRIDGE.

And so it would have been very surprising if the people who looked at my pictures somehow *missed* the incredible mountain view, and instead focused on the bottom corner of one of my photos and said, "Wow! Look at the little molehill!"

MOUNTAINS OVER MOLEHILLS

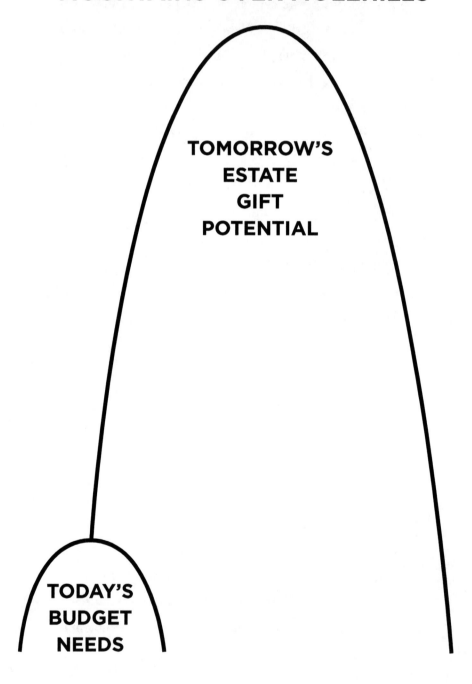

**TOMORROW'S
ESTATE
GIFT
POTENTIAL**

**TODAY'S
BUDGET
NEEDS**

But that's actually how it feels sometimes talking to ministry leaders. The entire focus of their fundraising and marketing teams is simply to run a little faster than last year so that they can raise a little more money to meet this year's increased budget goal.

The "molehill" in this picture is the potential pool of cash gifts people can make from their checkbooks and bank accounts today, and the "mountain" is the much larger potential pool of estate gifts in the background — from *the same donors!*

MOST MINISTRIES ARE CHASING THE "MOLEHILL" OF THIS YEAR'S BUDGET AND MISSING THE "MOUNTAIN" OF THEIR ESTATE GIFT POTENTIAL.

There are many good reasons why ministries spend more time chasing the "molehills" instead of climbing the "mountains." We'll address a few of the most common reasons in the Frequently Asked Questions section, but let's focus our attention on the mountain first.

If your deep desire is to look beyond the cash gift "molehills" to see the "mountains" of estate gifts, there are three game-changing mega-trends I believe you should really digest, and reflect on, and pray about:

Wealth. As I've previously stated, but need to repeat here, we've just entered the largest generational transfer of wealth in history. Let that monumental reality sink in a minute.

God placed *you* in the ministry of development at the *exact moment* in history when experts are saying that between now and 2050, somewhere between $30 to $60 trillion will change hands from this generation to the next. That's *trillion* dollars with a *"T."* None of us, myself included, can really grasp how enormous that is.

GOD PLACED YOU WHERE YOU ARE DURING THE LARGEST GENERATIONAL TRANSFER OF WEALTH IN HISTORY.

Let me try and break it down this way. If you could somehow spend $10 *million* per day, it would take you over *eight thousand years* to spend $30 trillion (and that's using the *low*-end estimate of the generational wealth transfer we're in right now).

Here's why this matters to you. When one of your faithful donors dies, their assets enter that massive $30 trillion transfer of wealth from this generation to the next.

How do you know if you can expect any of that wealth transfer to come to you? Well, keep in mind there are only three places their money can go: the government (estate taxes), family (kids and grandkids), and charity (that's you!). A very tiny percentage of estates are actually subject to tax, so that leaves "family" and "charity" as the only viable options for the vast majority of your donors.

Understandably, most people want to make sure their families are well taken care of. But did you know that many of those same people would be happy to also include your ministry in their Will as one of their "kids?"

For example, if one of your donors has three children, and your ministry gets added as a fourth "child" in their will, you'll receive 25 percent of their estate (that's a big deal, by the way!). This practice is sometimes referred to as "A Child Called Charity."

> MANY DONORS WOULD BE HAPPY TO INCLUDE YOUR MINISTRY IN THEIR WILL AS ONE OF THEIR KIDS.

But wait, it gets even better — about 10-15 percent of your faithful supporters have *no children*, and so for most of these fine folks with no estate taxes and no family inheritances they only have *one* option — to give *all* of their estate to ministry (and yes, that could be *you*!).

Hopefully, you're beginning to see that the opportunity to start or accelerate your movement into this historic flow of wealth is urgent and enormous!

Witness. More people need Jesus than ever before. The number of un-evangelized people around the world is rising rapidly — over 2 billion people with no exposure to Christ, and that number is expected to grow as the world population continues to expand.

To be fair, the *percentage* of un-evangelized people in the world has actually been dropping — from a little more than 50 percent of the world's population in 1900 to under 30 percent today. And that is great news! It's something we should praise the Lord for, and acknowledge the faithful witness of those who came before us — including missionaries, pastors, evangelists, and ordinary believers.

WHY CLIMB THIS MOUNTAIN? MORE PEOPLE NEED JESUS THAN EVER BEFORE.

But, the reality is there is a staggering amount of work still to be done and ministry opportunities to pursue. The harvest is ripe and the workers are few.

I know this message rings true in your heart like it does in mine. We don't see our work as just a "job" but rather as a calling and conviction to unleash the gifts God has given us to make a difference in the world for Christ. Well, guess what . . . *Many of your donors feel the same as you and me.*

Your donors sense that the world needs Jesus more now than ever before. And by supporting your ministry with their hard-earned dollars, they're saying they think you are on to something — that you're an important part of the solution.

Now is the time to show them the connection between their faithful support and your solution to the world's great need for Christ, especially as we move through this unique moment in history when the need for witnesses has never been greater.

Worship. One of the most amazing breakthrough discoveries the Money for Ministry team has made, is that for ministry-minded donors, estate planning — and specifically estate gifts — are an *act of worship*, not just a legal transaction or financial maneuver.

We have surveyed thousands and thousands of faithful donors about their possible interest in leaving a legacy for their families and the ministries they love. When we've asked people about their motivation for giving (and why they might even consider an estate gift), the answers were quite frankly a bit surprising at first.

> ESTATE GIFTS ARE AN ACT OF WORSHIP, NOT JUST A LEGAL TRANSACTION OR FINANCIAL MANEUVER.

Decades of planned gift marketing materials were built around the premise that donors are motivated by tax savings. That's why you see so many graphs and charts and painfully boring explanations of how various planned gift tools work, and how these tools can save donors money on their taxes.

Well it turns out most donors don't care about that. A minuscule percentage of donors even qualify to pay estate taxes.

What the majority of estate givers *do* care about, we've found, is their passion for God — which reflects a heart of *worship*. They acknowledge that God has blessed their lives and their families, and in that spirit, they are open to considering an offering of thanks back to God in the form of an estate gift.

CONNECT WITH THE WORSHIP MOTIVATION THAT DRIVES THE MAJORITY OF YOUR ESTATE GIFT PROSPECTS.

For many, this act of worship will, by far, be their largest gift ever. It reflects a lifetime of working and saving and raising a family and growing in their faith.

I believe this discovery (that estate gifts are an act of worship) builds on other research we've seen that found the most generous givers are not necessarily the wealthiest givers, but rather the people who are most faithful in Bible reading and prayer.

And now here we stand, together with you, full of anticipation and joy, as we watch God raising up a generation of Romans 12 givers, who see their bodies, lives and their estates as living sacrifices, holy and acceptable to God, their spiritual act of worship. For more on how to effectively speak into the worship motivation, you'll want to use the language of inspiration before information (see Chapter 2).

FREQUENTLY ASKED QUESTIONS

 We need money now so "planned giving" will have to wait.

(Notice this is actually a comment and not a question. But this is how it is usually put to us . . . It's also "molehill" thinking.)

With a serious "we mean business" expression on their face, and a hint of panic and stress in their voice, development staff tell us they feel like they're on a treadmill, running with all of their might to raise more money this year than last year to meet their increased goal.

They get paid to hit a certain goal, and as wonderful as "planned giving" is, it's seen as a potential distraction that's going to have to wait.

Sound familiar?

I want to encourage you from the *bottom of my heart* to stop for a moment and see that if you keep doing what you're doing, you will keep getting similar results, and that anxious "behind the eight ball" feeling you feel now will *never* go away.

Budgets and revenue targets will keep going up. The cost of doing ministry will continue to rise. And all of this will happen as the number of donors in your database may actually *shrink* over the next decade.

Now, bear in mind that shrinkage is not going to happen because you're necessarily doing anything wrong. It's just the reality of the demographic pattern we're in right now.

The majority of your current donors are part of the Baby Boomer generation. They are a very large group. The generation coming right behind them is called Gen X, and that generation is significantly smaller. That means if you haven't already, you will very likely soon notice that you have a noticeably smaller pool of donors to draw from for current dollars. This major demographic challenge is at your doorstep and requires very bold and big action.

In response, I want to urge you to start with prayer — real, passionate mountain-moving prayer — because prayer takes the enormous challenges you face with rising costs and revenue targets and shrinking donor bases, and puts it *all* in the mighty hands of God. The same hands that stretched out the incomprehensible galaxies, and made the heavens and the earth, and every living creature and person created in the image of God.

ESTATE GIFTS ARE THE SOLUTION TO YOUR SHRINKING DONOR BASE AND INCREASING COSTS.

Then recognize that "planned giving" isn't something nice you hope to get serious about someday when you have more time or budget. Instead, it's the mission-critical solution you need *today* to breathe a little easier - not only to address your "money now" challenges, but also to lay a strong and vibrant foundation for growth that will someday soon, Lord willing, lessen the pressure you feel to scramble every year to raise enough funds for current operations.

How can "planned giving" help you, your team and your ministry breathe easier *today* and in the years to come? In the previous chapter, I explained that you have a mountain of untapped "hidden" major gift potential sitting idle in your donor database right now (see Chapter 4 FAQ "Why do you call these little donors our 'hidden' major donors?"). Start there.

Then give this the *same urgency and priority* that you have given to your other "tried and true" development activities.

You'll know you're on the right track when planned giving is no longer an optional "someday" accessory that gets bolted on to

> INTEGRATE "PLANNED GIVING" INTO EVERYTHING YOU DO TO INFUSE NEW LIFE AND GROWTH IN YOUR MINISTRY.

your development program. But rather it becomes part of your team's DNA, infusing *new life* and *new growth* into *everything* you do — including your mail appeals, your online presence, your event strategy, and your engagement with mid-level and major donors.

Q Are endowment funds a good way to offset our rising costs and increased fundraising needs?

The Money for Ministry team gets a fair amount of questions and interest about endowments. There are three important questions you need to consider in order to decide if an endowment fund is the best way for your ministry to address future budget challenges:

Should you even have an endowment fund? Most ministries distinguish between cash reserves for short-term financial needs and endowment funds for long-term financial challenges. And most donors would agree and even expect you would have some cash reserves as an "insurance policy" to protect against short-term financial fluctuations.

But we've found that ministries and donors are split almost evenly down the middle, however, when it comes to endowments.

One half thinks endowment funds are smart and wise stewardship, helping to keep rising operational costs down over the long haul. Christian schools and colleges, for example, often rely on this approach to decrease their future tuition costs.

The other half of the ministry and donor world do not like endowment funds. They think it's best to spend down large donations such as estate gifts over a short period of time for ministry purposes.

For this group, there is often an expressed urgency to do all we can to advance the Gospel sooner rather than later, as well as a concern that one day when the Lord returns there will be huge sums of money sitting in endowment funds that could have been released for kingdom impact.

> DECIDE IN ADVANCE HOW YOU WILL TREAT LARGE ESTATE GIFTS: LONG-TERM ENDOWMENT STRATEGY OR SHORT-TERM "SPEND DOWN."

I don't believe there is a "right" answer to whether or not a ministry should have an endowment. We work with wonderful sincere believers connected to fruitful ministries on both sides of this debate. But I wanted to outline the two positions for you, so that you and your leadership can prayerfully come to your own conclusion.

If you have an endowment fund, how do you set a goal for it? The answer depends on what *source* you plan to pursue to fund your endowment.

If you plan to pursue major gifts as your source (ex. current cash or asset-based gifts from major donors), then coming up with the "right" number is similar to a major gift campaign. You'd begin with an informal feasibility study to gauge the interest among your major donors who might contribute to your endowment fund, and the gift range they might consider.

With this approach, you are rooting your endowment fund goals and projections in actual donor interest and their capacity to give. On the other hand, if you plan to pursue estate gifts as the primary source to fund your endowment, then coming up with a goal will require a little research and math:

> *How many donors have already told you they*
> *   included your ministry in their Will?*
> *What is the average size estate gift you've received*
> *   over the past 5 years?*
> *How many new estate gifts and interested prospects is*
> *   your current strategy producing?*
> *If that pattern continued for the next 5-10 years, what*
> *   could you reasonably project for new estate gifts*
> *   and prospects in that time frame?*
> *If you have age information on your donors and*
> *   prospects, can you estimate the timing of these*
> *   estate gifts?*

How will you communicate current needs to donors if you have millions in your endowment? The underlying and very common concern most ministries have is that estate gifts and endowment funds will discourage current giving.

An executive director reached out to me recently to ask, "If our budget need this year is $10 million, and we have $20 million in our endowment fund, how can we tell our donors 'we need money'?" My answer to him (and to you) is that you need to consider *who* would benefit from knowing that you have "$20 million in the bank."

DETERMINE HOW YOU WILL PURSUE ENDOWMENT FUND GROWTH: MAJOR GIFTS, ESTATE GIFTS, OR BOTH.

Three groups that would likely appreciate hearing about the strength of your endowment fund are your known estate givers, your emerging estate gift prospects, and of course anyone who cares enough to read or request your annual report.

Unlike traditional major donors that often like to give to projects and campaigns, estate givers are typically giving to your overall "big picture" mission. And so for many, a healthy endowment fund gives them confidence you will be around for a long time, because you have laid a solid foundation for future growth.

Then for your donors responding to your ongoing solicitations in the mail and online, you shouldn't feel an obligation to advertise your $20 million endowment balance in that donor communication channel. Their primary interest is that their gift of $100 is being used to help someone in need today. They typically assume you are managing your finances wisely. If they didn't believe that, they'd either do some research or stop giving.

 ## When are we going to start seeing results?

It is very possible to see results from your estate gift program sooner rather than later.

But you'll want to first define what kind of results you're looking for because, "if you aim at nothing, you'll hit it every time." Having a clear goal matters.

If you want to see estate gift results, step one is to prayerfully establish a compelling goal, one that:

- *Sets the stage for very satisfying results. It reminds you that only God can accomplish something so enormous.*
- *Reminds you and your team that maximum estate gift growth is a marathon, not a sprint.*
- *Unifies and energizes your team around a common purpose to be everything God intends for you and your ministry.*
- *Lets you know if you're on track or not as you follow God's leading in this exciting adventure.*

There will be multiple distractions that will try and pull you away from your goal. You will face "competing" priorities (ex. getting the next mailing out the door, updating your website, organizing events, connecting with your major donors, etc.).

You will face momentary lulls in the action when it appears your estate gift momentum is slowing down. This is normal, and it's why it's so mission critical that you set a compelling goal first. It will help you and your team navigate through these uncomfortable but predictable situations, stay the course, and continue to ride the wave into more estate gifts and deeper donor relationships than ever before.

> IF YOU FOCUS ON THE MOLE HILL YOU WILL MISS THE MOUNTAIN.

What are you aiming for over the next 5-10 years? You really need to start with a "big picture" question like this, if for no other reason than to remind yourself, your team, your boss and your board that maximum estate gift growth is a mountain, not a molehill.

If you focus on the "molehill" (did we get any estate gifts in the door yet this quarter?), you will miss the "mountain" (are we creating an environment to maximize the estate gift potential in our *entire* donor file?).

Every ministry is unique and approaches estate gift goal-setting differently. But the first question *every* ministry should ask is "What should *our* goal be?" I can't answer that for you, but I can help lead you to the right answer by the end of this chapter.

Another way to ask this critical question is, what result do you believe the Lord wants to accomplish through your ministry? We can't answer your "when will we see results?" question until we know what *specific* result you are aiming for.

WHAT RESULT DOES THE LORD WANT TO ACCOMPLISH THROUGH YOU? WHAT IS YOUR COMPELLING GOAL?

So what I'll do here is lay out the three most common kinds of "results" ministries tell us they are seeking. Then I'd encourage you to reflect a bit on the list, pray about it, and see if one or more of these resonate with your heart, to help you establish a goal you believe is God's will for your ministry.

Result #1: New estate gift donors. Newly discovered estate gift donors are the "low hanging fruit." They already included you in their Will; they just haven't told you yet. But you need those early "wins" to build your momentum. Then you can expand your pool of new estate givers over time, and ultimately increase the engagement with your ministry — now and into the future.

New estate gift donors are probably the most common goal ministries set because it's pretty straight-forward: how many new estate gift commitments did we get this year?

Most ministries may actually *prefer* to set a dollar amount goal, but that can be tricky because so many estate gift donors choose not to disclose that. So they opt instead to set a goal they can more easily measure.

To give you an idea of how this process works, here's an overview of how one of our national ministry clients arrived at their estate gift goal. Their historical estate gift average was just north of $50,000, so they determined they would need 20,000 estate gift donors to reach their goal.

They observed that historically, about 20 percent of their estate gift donors reported the gift in advance, and the other 80 percent of estate gifts they had received, despite their best efforts, were never reported, but were received with gratitude when those "surprise" checks came in.

NEWLY DISCOVERED ESTATE GIFT DONORS ARE THE "LOW HANGING FRUIT" YOU NEED TO BUILD YOUR MOMENTUM AND EXPAND YOUR POOL OF NEW ESTATE GIVERS OVER TIME.

If the 80/20 pattern held, they could reasonably conclude that of the 20,000 estate gift donors they'd need to reach their goal, about 80 percent (16,000 donors) would be influenced by the ministry's proactive estate gift marketing over time, but would never report their gift.

And about 20 percent (4,000 donors) would be needed to not only take action, but also be willing to report their estate gift decision to the ministry.

They already knew about 500 estate gifts on file. Consequently, they set a goal to surface 3,500 *new* reported estate gifts over the next 10 years (4,000 reported estate gifts needed minus 500 existing reported gifts equals 3,500 reported estate gifts to reach their goal).

> IF 20% OF DONORS REPORT THEIR ESTATE GIFT TO THE MINISTRY, HOW MANY WOULD BE NEEDED TO REACH THE GOAL?

Did you follow that? I hope so. But if not, let me offer another pretty simple way that ministries use to measure their number of estate gift donors.

Ministries sometimes will calculate the percentage of their donors that are known estate givers. Forgive me for getting a little nerdy on you, but we call this their "conversion ratio." For example, if a ministry has 30,000 donors, and they have 300 reported estate gifts on file, their "conversion ratio" is 1 percent.

The conversion ratio can vary widely by ministry. Some ministries are just getting started, so their conversion ratio is zero. Others have been at it for a little while and are approaching 1 percent. We see other ministries with an established estate gift marketing program or a strong affinity with their donor file in the 3-5 percent range.

The highest we've seen so far is 12 percent, which means for every 100 active donors, 12 of them have confirmed an estate gift with the ministry. There is no "one size fits all" conversion ratio for every ministry.

WHAT PERCENTAGE OF YOUR ACTIVE DONORS HAVE NOTIFIED YOU OF AN ESTATE GIFT?

If you resonate with the challenge of increasing the percentage of donors who are known estate givers, I would encourage you to calculate what your conversion ratio is today. Then decide what a reasonable target percentage would be for your ministry to achieve, say one year from now, and five years from now.

Result #2: New prospects. Other ministries want to see waves of faithful donors popping up with new interest to say they are now potentially interested in leaving a legacy to their families and the ministries they love. These "hot leads" create many new open doors for you to serve your donors well.

And if you use the dialogue approach we recommended in Chapter 2, you'll receive a steady flow of fresh insights, comments, and prayer requests from those newly surfaced estate gift prospects to help you build those relationships.

As your new prospects begin to raise their hands, the big key will be to "serve not sell" them (see Chapter 3). If donors feel free to tell you they would consider an estate gift to your ministry, or need help creating or updating their Will, or want more information, that's a very positive signal as they are now bringing you into their life as a trusted friend and partner.

WHEN SOMEONE RESPONDS TO YOUR ESTATE GIFT "DIALOGUE", THEY ARE INVITING YOU INTO THEIR LIFE AS A TRUSTED FRIEND AND MINISTRY PARTNER.

We find that the ministries most interested in setting a "new prospects" goal generally have a donor rep or team who are eager to meet with interested donors. And often, they have been using a variety of common but ineffective approaches to generate new leads and are dissatisfied.

For example, one ministry called us to say they were cold calling their donors to see if they could get anyone to talk to them about estate gifts. As you can imagine, that was not well received by the donors, so they called to ask about fresh, proven approaches for surfacing new and interested prospects, along with some perspective on how to set realistic goals.

Another ministry called to say they were relying on a turnkey website and email program to generate new leads.

While this approach was providing a trickle of new interest, their team believed there was much more potential in their donor file, so they called us to help them reimagine what's possible and discuss a proven pathway to get there.

My advice to you, if you're interested in increasing the number of new prospects you are surfacing and engaging each year, is to begin by reviewing what we said in Chapter 2 about building a "Dialogue over Monologue" approach with your donors. From there you should be able to begin setting some realistic prospect goals, and if you need additional help, our team would be happy to assist you.

Result #3: New dollars. And now the result you *really* wanted to know about — the dollars. There are several ways ministries experience short-term dollar results in planned gift ministry. Some receive

> NEW PROSPECTS SHARING NEW INTEREST, COMMENTS, AND PRAYER REQUESTS CREATE MANY NEW OPEN DOORS FOR YOU TO SERVE YOUR DONORS WELL.

estate gifts sooner rather than later (often coming from your longtime faithful givers in their 80s and 90s).

Some see increases in current giving as people become more engaged with the estate gift conversation. Others send donor surveys and receive unsolicited cash gifts in return. Some even see gifts of appreciated stock and other asset-based gifts begin to surface as they promote giving beyond the checkbook.

I mentioned earlier that many ministries would like to set an estate gift dollar amount goal, but some end up not doing that when they realize how many estate gift donors choose not to disclose their gift amount, or don't know what the amount will be, given it's a percentage of *what's left* in the estate after they pass away. So needless to say, it's challenging to set an estate gift dollar goal.

> THERE ARE MANY WAYS THAT ESTATE GIFT MARKETING PRODUCES NEW DOLLARS NOW — INCLUDING ESTATE GIFTS FROM OLDER DONORS, INCREASES IN CURRENT GIVING, AND ASSET-BASED GIFTS.

But ministries still do this, often because their boss or board wants a number (even an estimate) to get a sense of how they're doing.

The way some ministries approach this is by doing everything they can to encourage as many donors as possible to disclose a dollar amount. This happens in face to face meetings with donors, sometimes connected to capital campaign interviews. We've also used donor surveys to facilitate this kind of information exchange, and if handled with care, this too can be very effective.

But for the vast majority of estate gift donors, they will unfortunately *not* disclose a dollar amount. There are a variety of reasons for this, but for many it often comes down to privacy and uncertainty about the future. So what do you do?

If your team is being asked to provide dollar amounts, and you have precious few donors willing to disclose dollar amounts, then you can provide estimates, provided you are very clear in your communications that your numbers are estimates based on the best available data you have.

> MOST ESTATE GIFT DONORS DO NOT DISCLOSE A DOLLAR AMOUNT BECAUSE OF PRIVACY CONCERNS AND UNCERTAINTY ABOUT THE FUTURE.

A large, nationally-recognized ministry recently contacted our team to ask for help reaching their dollar estate gift goal. They had calculated the historical average size of their estate gifts by looking at the past 5-10 years of donor data, and they knew how many new estate gifts they wanted to surface in order to reach their dollar goal.

If you have records of past estate gifts on file, the chances are pretty good that the gift amounts will vary widely. That's totally normal. Going forward, the chances are also pretty good that this pattern will repeat.

So go ahead and do the math. And if your average estate gift comes out to say $47,000, then you can use that number to project that if you get 100 more estate gifts over the next 10 years, based on your own historical data, the *estimated* value of those estate gifts could be approximately $4.7 million.

YOU CAN PRODUCE ESTATE GIFT ESTIMATES USING YOUR HISTORICAL DATA AND NATIONAL AVERAGES.

That's the math this national ministry was using. And you can do the same, provided you are very clear in your communication with your leadership and team that this is just an estimate based on your historical estate gift data.

If you don't have good data on past estate gifts (and many ministries don't), then we suggest using a national average. Again, estate gifts can vary widely by ministry type and size, but we've found that a pretty good average across all ministries is right around $50,000.

That number appears to be trending up, and it includes the smaller estate gifts that come in under $10,000, as well as the 6-figure and 7-figure estate gifts, but it gives you a reasonable starting point if you're asked to come up with some estimates.

One final thought on estate gift results. It's something I want to bring up that ministry leaders rarely talk about or if they do, say it jokingly.

They say something like, "If I bust my rear end and do a great job tilling the soil and planting the seeds, and a wave of huge estate gifts come in years after I'm gone, the *next person* will get the credit for it!"

If you've said that, or thought that, it's OK. *Everyone* has thought that to some degree.

Let me encourage you with two thoughts here. First, if you truly believe in the mission of your organization, and want to see it become everything God wants it to be, then you can go "all in" with planned gift ministry and not care who gets the credit.

> GO "ALL IN" WITH ESTATE GIFT MARKETING BECAUSE IT'S THE BEST AND RIGHT THING TO DO, REGARDLESS OF WHO GETS THE CREDIT.

Hopefully a lot of those dollars will come in while you are still there. Many of those dollars may come in after you've moved on. But just remember what's at stake here: eternal ministry impact . . . millions of new dollars . . . helping your most faithful donors experience this special act of worship.

So let me just assure you that I understand you rightfully need to get some "credit" now for your labors in the real world of performance evaluations and reports to bosses and boards. Re-read what I said earlier about results and you will see there are numerous ways you will get credit *now* for your efforts, as you faithfully and passionately invest in the tremendous opportunities to also receive "results later."

RECAP

HOW TO RIDE THE WAVE OF MOUNTAINS OVER MOLEHILLS

Most ministries are chasing "molehills", running a little faster to raise a little more money than last year, and missing the "mountain" of estate gift potential from the same pool of donors.

Commit today to start or accelerate your climb up the mountain of the greatest generational transfer of wealth in history.

Remind yourself why you are climbing the mountain: more people need Jesus than ever before.

Connect with the worship motivation that drives the majority of your estate gift prospects.

Integrate "planned giving" into everything you do to infuse new life and growth in your ministry.

Decide in advance how you will treat large estate gifts: long-term endowment strategy or short-term "spend down."

Determine how you will pursue endowment fund growth: major gifts, estate gifts, or both.

What result does the Lord want to accomplish through you? If you aim at nothing, you'll hit it every time.

Newly discovered estate gift donors are the "low hanging fruit" you need to build your momentum and expand your pool of new estate givers over time.

New prospects sharing new interest, comments, and prayer requests create many new open doors for you to serve your donors well.

There are many ways that estate gift marketing produces new dollars now, including estate gifts from older donors, increases in current giving, and asset-based gifts.

Go "all in" with estate gift marketing because it's the best and right thing to do regardless of who gets the credit.

WHAT'S WORKING
A COMPELLING GOAL

" When we calculated our estate gift growth potential and realized it was $1 billion, we did not hesitate for a moment. We remembered that Joshua prayed to God to make the sun stand still because he knew that God could do the impossible. This is not about our capabilities or what we think is possible. We can clearly see that the Lord is in this. His strength and what He can achieve through those He calls is our motivation."

Lisa Reschetnikow
ADF Foundation
Serving Alliance Defending Freedom

CLOSING THOUGHTS
WAVES OF JOY

5 Keys to Ride the Wave Now

I set my luggage and laptop down for just a minute as I looked up at the arrivals and departures screen in the airport, right next to a very busy bar and grill.

I breathed a sigh of relief when I realized I had just over an hour to get to my plane. My gate was located at the other end of the airport, but no worries, I had plenty of time.

I could relax a bit and enjoy a leisurely stroll through the airport. I noticed a sunglasses shop staffed by a female clerk with oversized neon-green sunglasses. Up ahead was a food court with people scurrying through who clearly did not have the luxury of time I was relishing.

The smells of roast beef sandwiches on artisan buns met the equally tempting aromas of sweet-and-sour chicken with fried rice. Both options looked and smelled delicious, but I wasn't really very hungry, so I decided to keep moseying along.

I stepped on to several of those moving walkways, as I made progress towards my gate. Along the way, I passed a few parents with their kids, which made me all the more eager to get home and see my own family.

I finally arrived at my gate with over a half hour to spare. I settled into a nice open seat by the window, positioned my luggage as a foot rest, reached for my laptop . . . My laptop!

Where was my *laptop*? My peaceful state of bliss turned to *panic*! I *need* my laptop, and I have *no idea* where it is. And I began to wonder if someone else may have already run off with it.

> MY PEACEFUL STATE OF BLISS TURNED TO PANIC WHEN I REALIZED I DIDN'T HAVE MY LAPTOP.

But there was no time to worry. Like a bolt of lightning, I shot down the concourse to backtrack my exact route through the entire airport, knowing I must return to this gate in about 30 minutes.

But this time I wasn't admiring the happy families ambling through the airport in their Disney T-shirts and flip-flops. This time I didn't see or smell the deli sandwiches or Asian buffet options (I did however notice the girl with the oversized neon-green sunglasses again — impossible to miss her!).

And then I finally returned to the original spot where I last remembered having my laptop — the "arrivals and departures" screen next to the bustling open air bar and grill. I scanned the area where I had been standing. No laptop, anywhere.

I went over to one of the wait staff and asked in desperation if he'd happened to see my laptop. My heart sank as he apologized and said he hadn't seen it. His manager, however, overheard our brief exchange and asked, "Did you say laptop? Are you missing a laptop?"

"Yes," I replied feeling a very small spark of hope light up inside of me.

"I found one here a little while ago and turned it over to the airport police," he began. "If it's yours you'll need to go back through security, up the elevator, and go claim it in their office."

I thanked him and sprinted away like I was trying to qualify for the 400-meter dash. When I arrived at the police station, they confirmed they had just received a laptop, but I would need to describe it in detail in order for them to turn it over to me.

"OK, no problem," I said, trying to catch my breath so I could speak. "Black case with red stripe. Outer pocket with a tin of cinnamon Altoid breath mints and a notepad. Inside the case is my MacBook Pro with a maroon protective case. And if you flip it open, you'll see a picture of my wife and me and our kids on the screen."

> I THANKED THE MAN AND SPRINTED AWAY LIKE I WAS TRYING TO QUALIFY FOR THE 400-METER DASH.

With a big smile on her face, the desk clerk handed me my laptop and said "have a nice day." Waves of joy washed over me as I responded with, "Thank you! I feel like you just saved my life."

Does my reaction seem a bit over the top? Well maybe it depends: have *you* ever lost your laptop? Or smart phone? Or purse? Or wallet? If so, you know it's one of the most horrible, sinking feelings in the world.

And if you don't end up finding it, it's a HUGE hassle to get your credit cards, driver's license, and health care cards re-issued. Same goes for getting a new device and then attempting to reassemble your key documents and upload your contacts.

Why is this such a big deal? It's because our lives are wrapped up in these things. Like a combination to a safe, there are at least five basic items that you carry with you everywhere that "unlock the door" of opportunity in your daily life:

- **Your driver's license** unlocks your ability to drive a car
- **Your bank cards** unlock your access to your money
- **Your contact file** unlocks your connections to people in your life
- **Your medical cards** unlock your health care options
- **Your devices** allow you to communicate and create with family and colleagues

If you're missing any of these five things, you feel anxious, maybe even a bit terrified. There's an ache in your stomach because you know something is missing and you want to resolve it. But if you *have* these five things, and *use* these five things, they unlock the door to a wealth of opportunities, relationships, and joy in your life.

The very same dynamic is at work with your ministry's enormous estate potential. Your ministry is poised for a whole new level of opportunities, relationships, and waves of joy — for you, your team, and the donors you serve. And the reason this is true, now more than ever, is because God has set the stage for the largest generational transfer of wealth and worship in history.

> IF YOU HAVE THESE FIVE THINGS, THEY UNLOCK THE DOOR TO A WEALTH OF OPPORTUNITY AND JOY IN YOUR LIFE.

And just like your driver's license, bank cards, contact file, healthcare cards, and devices "unlock" the doors of opportunity in your daily life, our team at Money for Ministry has found, over and over again, that there are also five keys that unlock the door to your ministry's full estate gift potential. Those five keys are:

Key #1: A Goal to Keep You Going

What result does the Lord want to accomplish through you and your ministry? Well, if you aim at nothing, you'll hit it every time. But a specific goal to surface estate gift donors builds your momentum and expands your pool of opportunities and relationships.

A goal to engage new prospects will open new doors of conversation, prayer requests, relationship building, and estate gift interest. A goal to increase giving now can be accomplished with estate gifts from older donors, increased giving from cultivated estate givers which can for some include asset-based gifts such as stocks, retirement savings, real estate, and more.

> **IF YOU AIM AT NOTHING, YOU'LL HIT IT EVERY TIME.**

Boldly go "all in" with estate gift marketing, because it's the best and right thing to do regardless of who gets the credit. See the FAQ in Chapter 5 for more on goal setting.

Key #2: Your Message for the Masses

Start with your *existing* donor communication channels (ex. print, digital, events, personal contacts) to reach all of your donors, all of the time.

Remember that your donors need some *inspiration* first, then if they're interested, give them the how-to *information*. The two things that inspire ministry-minded donors most are their *families* and (if they're believers) their *faith* in Christ.

So use messaging that speaks to these motivations. Your aim is to create content that inspires *responders* rather than informs *readers*. Offer to *give* people something on your response cards — not just *ask* them for something. Replace *jargon* like "planned giving" or "bequest" with clear *everyday words* like "gift in my Will." See Chapter 1 for more on engaging the masses with your messaging.

Key #3: Your Interaction with the Interested

Treat your planned gift messaging like a warm conversation with friends rather than a commercial you broadcast to faceless strangers.

That conversation should lead the donor through three steps that every estate giver takes: *awareness* (speaking into the desires, needs, and fears your donor is experiencing), *interest* (listening to the donor's preferences, comments, and prayer requests), and *action* (offering easy-to-understand "next step" information).

We recommend an interactive survey program to kick-start the conversation, but only if there is a solid follow-up system in place to serve interested donors.

Finally, develop a plan that engages your entire donor file over time in the planned gift ministry dialogue. See Chapter 2 for more on *how* to engage interested donor prospects, and Chapter 4 for more on *who* your best prospects are.

Key #4: Your Connection with the Committed

Treat your known estate givers like major donors.

It doesn't matter if a donor is currently giving $50 or $5,000 per year. If they *committed* a gift to you in their Will, and took the time to *connect* with you to tell you about it, it's time to add them to your major donor list. A gift of $50,000 may be on the way. Love them well.

When they are making their final Will revision at age 80, don't give them a reason to take your ministry off their list. Build the relationship with a semi-annual Legacy Society newsletter. Host special events to thank them, build community, and encourage interested prospects to join in the excitement. Reach out to them by phone or in person to thank them for their gift (even if it's $10). See Chapter 3 for more on how to build the relationship with your growing pool of known estate givers.

Key #5: Your Traction with Your Team

For optimal estate gift growth, teamwork makes the dream work.

No more silos. Cast a vision for your team that estate gifts are a huge game-changing priority (see my section on Wealth, Witness, and Worship in Chapter 5). Integrate your estate gift message naturally and seamlessly with all team members and across all communication channels (ex. receipts, direct mail program, newsletters, website, event strategy, and existing personal donor contacts).

Tap into the expertise of gift planners (ex. National Christian Foundation, Barnabas Foundation, Orchard Foundation, MB Foundation, etc.). And if you have questions about how to set up a marketing program that surfaces new interest and new estate gifts, our team at Money for Ministry is happy to help. See the FAQ section in Chapter 3 for more on effective teamwork.

If you prayerfully take action on these five proven and ministry-tested keys above, you can unlock the door to your ministry's full estate gift potential.

> GOD IS THE WAVE AND HE WANTS TO DO SOMETHING INCREDIBLE THROUGH YOUR MINISTRY.

You can "ride the wave" into more estate gifts than ever before.

You can minister to the hearts of more donors like never before.

God is the wave, and He wants to use the themes you read about in the previous chapters — Inspiration, Dialogue, Serving, Widows, and Mountains — to do something incredible through you!

This is your moment.

Let's go!

RIDE THE WAVE
GAME PLAN

1. **GOAL** that keeps you going.

---

2. **MESSAGE** for the masses.

---

3. **INTERACT** with your interested prospects.

---

4. **CONNECT** with your committed estate gift donors.

---

5. **TRACTION** with your team.

WHAT'S WORKING
INTEGRATED GROWTH PLAN

" The integration of planned giving into all of our revenue and communication streams is important because we consider it to be a tremendous ministry opportunity for our donors and other constituents, regardless of the amount they give or channel they give through. We also believe that current giving and planned giving go hand-in-hand in faithful biblical stewardship."

George Fisher

Wycliffe Bible Translators USA

READY TO RIDE THE WAVE?

 **Go to moneyforministry.com and click "Free Report"**

 **You'll receive a free, no-obligation summary of:**

- Your estate gift potential
- A customized 5-step program to get you there
- Service options tailored to your needs and budget

MONEYFORMINISTRY

HELPING MINISTRIES GROW SINCE 2003

MORE BOOKS?

Share this message with your:
- Team
- Leadership
- Board Members
- Ministry Friends

www.moneyforministry.com/freebook

Contact your friends at Money for Ministry:
info@moneyforministry.com
(616) 723-8369